MW00856653

THE 5 DISCIPLINES OF INCLUSIVE TEAMS

The Five Inclusive Disciplines trilogy, with primary research by the authors and The Korn Ferry Institute, includes

The 5 Disciplines of Inclusive Leaders: Unleashing the Power of All of Us by Andrés Tapia and Alina Polonskaia (Berrett-Koehler, 2020)

The 5 Disciplines of Inclusive Organizations: How Diverse and Equitable Enterprises Will Transform the World by Andrés Tapia and Fayruz Kirtzman (Berrett-Koehler, 2023)

The 5 Disciplines of Inclusive Teams: Unlocking Collective Power to Achieve Breakthrough by Andrés T. Tapia and Michel Buffet, PhD (Berrett-Koehler, 2025)

THE 5 DISCIPLINES OF INCLUSIVE TEAMS

Unlocking Collective Power to Achieve Breakthrough

ANDRÉS T. TAPIA & MICHEL BUFFET, PhD

BK

Berrett–Koehler Publishers, Inc.

Copyright © 2025 by Korn Ferry, Andrés T. Tapia and Michel Buffet PhD
The Inclusive™ is a trademark of Korn Ferry.

All rights reserved. No portion of this work may be reproduced or transmitted in any form or by any means, electronic or mechanical, including photocopying and recording, or by any information storage or retrieval system, or be used in training generative artificial intelligence (AI) technologies or developing machine-learning language models without permission, except in the case of brief quotations embodied in critical reviews and certain other noncommercial uses permitted by copyright law. For permission requests, please contact the Copyright Clearance Center at marketplace.copyright.com/rs-ui-web/mp.

Berrett-Koehler Publishers, Inc.
1333 Broadway, Suite P100
Oakland, CA 94612–1921
Tel: (510) 817–2277
Fax: (510) 817–2278
bkconnection.com

ORDERING INFORMATION

Quantity sales. Special discounts are available on quantity purchases by corporations, associations, and others. For details, please go to bkconnection.com to see our bulk discounts or contact bookorders@bkpub.com for more information.

Individual sales. Berrett-Koehler publications are available through most bookstores. They can also be ordered directly from Berrett-Koehler: Tel: (800) 929–2929; Fax: (802) 864–7626; bkconnection.com.

Orders for college textbook / course adoption use. Please contact Berrett-Koehler: Tel: (800) 929–2929; Fax: (802) 864–7626.

Distributed to the US trade and internationally by Penguin Random House Publisher Services.

Berrett-Koehler and the BK logo are registered trademarks of Berrett-Koehler Publishers, Inc.

Printed in the United States of America

Berrett-Koehler books are printed on long-lasting acid-free paper. When it is available, we choose paper that has been manufactured by environmentally responsible processes. These may include using trees grown in sustainable forests, incorporating recycled paper, minimizing chlorine in bleaching, or recycling the energy produced at the paper mill.

Library of Congress Cataloging-in-Publication Data

Names: Tapia, Andrés, 1960– author. | Buffet, Michel, PhD, author.
Title: The 5 disciplines of inclusive teams : unlocking collective power
    to achieve breakthrough / Andrés T. Tapia, Michel Buffet.
Other titles: Unlocking collective power to achieve breakthrough
Description: First edition. | Oakland, CA : Berrett-Koehler Publishers, Inc.,
    [2025] | Series: The five disciplines trilogy ; 3 | Includes bibliographical
    references and index.
Identifiers: LCCN 2024038119 (print) | LCCN 2024038120 (ebook) |
    ISBN 9781523006465 (hardcover) | ISBN 9781523006472 (pdf) |
    ISBN 9781523006489 (epub)
Subjects: LCSH: Diversity in the workplace. | Teams in the workplace. | Leadership.
Classification: LCC HF5549.5.M5 T35 2025 (print) | LCC HF5549.5.M5 (ebook) |
    DDC 658.3008—dc23/eng/20241107
LC record available at https://lccn.loc.gov/2024038119
LC ebook record available at https://lccn.loc.gov/2024038120

First Edition

32 31 30 29 28 27 26 25 24   10 9 8 7 6 5 4 3 2 1

Book production: Westchester Publishing Services
Cover design: Dan Tesser
Author photos: Andrés Tapias: Diana Gran, Michel Buffet: Elizabeth Massa

To all the fútbol, work, volunteer, and leadership teams I have ever been a part of: We created transformative magic and there's more to come!

—Andrés

To my late father, Marcel Buffet, who gave me my first lessons in leadership and to my mother, Josefa Gomez, who taught me the importance of living with a caring heart and a curious mind.
To my children, Camille, Claude and Diane, whose purposeful endeavors and joyful spirits inspire me and fill me with pride.
To my husband, Marcin, for his unconditional love and support.

—Michel

"The strength of the team is each individual member. The strength of each member is the team."

—Phil Jackson
Six-time NBA championship coach
for the Chicago Bulls

CONTENTS

Contents

FOREWORD

A S AN ENTERPRISE-WIDE STRATEGIST, I focus on talent and corporate social responsibility, and their impact on business goals. Accordingly, I pay attention to data from a broad array of experts and to the insights from employees' experiences. Here's what I've observed (much like Andrés and Michel explain in this book): diverse teams, equitable systems, and an inclusive culture are the hallmarks of successful organizations. These are the organizations that consistently attract, engage, develop, and advance the best talent across a vast array of diversity, while at the same time impacting social justice in the community and growing revenues.

While working with multiple organizations and doing the research for my own book, *Leading Global Diversity, Equity, and Inclusion*, it became clear that aspirational statements by leaders are merely performative without the ability to live up to them through processes, policies, and programs. Rather, a systems approach, intentionality, and an inclusive culture that ensures all employees can contribute fully enable an organization's optimal success. Ensuring these elements were in place is what made the difference for organizations like Sodexo, where I was SVP corporate responsibility and global chief diversity officer, in terms of commercial success as well as brand strength.

In *The 5 Disciplines of Inclusive Teams*, Andrés and Michel are on to something very significant. There can be great ideas for improving policies, processes, and systems, and macro skilling and re-skilling as the world of work evolves, but ultimately, change happens at the intersection of people and processes. An organization's scaffolding and machinery—its processes—are *dependent on the ability of their diverse teams and their inclusive team leaders to make it all work*. Teams and their leaders are at the heart of it all.

While much has been written and practiced about what generally makes teams work well, there has been little exploration of how to make diverse and inclusive teams work optimally. It's true that there's a well-documented correlation between diverse teams and innovation, as well as between diversity and team effectiveness, but no one has quite figured out yet how that happens.

Until now.

Andrés and Michel state in their introduction that they set out to "crack the code" of this phenomenon. In this book, they reveal their research-based, insightful—and at times counterintuitive—findings. Best of all, these findings are always anchored in practical recommendations which can be implemented by any team of any size.

That the authors present their work through the framing of *disciplines* is telling. They recognize that, for teams to be effective, the right things can't just be done once in a while—they must be performed consistently, skillfully, and collaboratively. Then they go further and share the *practices* their research and field work told them are necessary building blocks for each of the disciplines.

Not only does their work resonate with me as I look back on my many years of experience, but also as I look forward in my ongoing work. Teams today have become more important than ever, especially since so many more teams now work remotely. As Andrés and Michel write, a major transformation is taking place. The days of top-down change are becoming outdated; change driven from the middle of the organization is the way of the future. This is because today's era of disruption requires fast, agile, and creative responses that can only happen with the full activation of diverse and inclusive teams.

It was not just this resonance that caught my attention, but also that the work came from Korn Ferry—an organization steeped in the science of talent—and from two deeply experienced practitioners and thought leaders: Andrés, whom I've known since we were both chief diversity officers in different organizations and whom I've seen bring his differentiated yet effective thinking and articulation to all types of audiences, seeking to solve a vast variety of organizational challenges, and Michel Buffet, whom I have not met personally but, through reading this book, I can see has significant experience in working with top executive teams in the world. It's clear he has gleaned powerful learnings that can now be applied to teams seeking to be inclusive at any level of their organizations.

You will find this book easy to read with strong storytelling, novel ideas, plenty of examples and case studies, and many practical steps which teams can implement to become the fully inclusive—and therefore the optimally innovative and effective—teams they aspire to be.

This book is a significant contribution to vital work that no organization can let up on.

Foreword by Rohini Anand, PhD, former Senior Vice President, Corporate Responsibility, and Global Chief Diversity Officer, Sodexo

■　　■　　■

PROLOGUE

WHAT MAKES DIVERSE AND INCLUSIVE TEAMS so much more effective?

The answer (and much more) lies in the pages to come, but first, it's important to know that this question is a follow-up to the one we asked in the first book of our Five Inclusive Disciplines trilogy:

What makes inclusive leaders so effective?

In that first book, *The 5 Disciplines of Inclusive Leaders: Unleashing the Power of All of Us*, we introduced our research-derived 5 Disciplines of Inclusive Leaders model. We unpacked how inclusive leaders increase their impact first by leading self, then by leading teams, and finally by leading their organizations in ways that address and leverage diversity, equity, and inclusion (DE&I). This first book focused on the dimension of leading self.

The second book, *The 5 Disciplines of Inclusive Organizations: How Diverse and Equitable Enterprises Will Transform the World*, presented leaders with the myriad benefits of having a diverse and inclusive organization—from more effective talent systems to better product/service/marketplace fits to a greater and more sustainable impact on their communities and the environment.

But inclusive leaders obviously don't make it happen alone. Because teams are the smallest unit of culture within organizations, it's the role of the inclusive leader to develop, nurture, and empower diverse and inclusive teams to achieve breakthrough. That's the focus of this third and final book in the Five Inclusive Disciplines trilogy.

For each of these books we mapped out five inclusive disciplines that turn intent into action at three levels: leader, organization, and team. We call them "disciplines" because fostering inclusion and activating it to achieve any number of organizational goals doesn't just happen through concept and rhetoric. It happens through practices applied conscientiously and consistently. Inclusive leaders, teams, and organizations develop habits that consistently and sustainably, rather than episodically, shape who they are and the impact they have on those around them.

We love and live these disciplines. In a personal high-stakes proof-of-concept move to showcase the power of diversity, equity, and inclusion, I, the founding author, invited different Korn Ferry colleagues to coauthor each book alongside me.

Each book in the trilogy is elevated in quality, depth of thought, examples, and practicalities because of the collaborative academic, creative, and application work we did across multiple forms of diversity. Starting with Andrés having grown up in a bilingual and bicultural home in Lima, Peru with a Peruvian Dad and an American Mom, plus with all the complexities that coauthoring entails, there is no way any of these books could have been completed on time—and with the relationships stronger by the end than at the beginning—without practicing full inclusion with one another!

The 5 Disciplines of Inclusive Leaders coauthor, Alina Polonskaia, is a Korn Ferry Senior Partner, CEO Succession and Enterprise Leadership. She played an integral role in the marketplace outreach and commercialization of The Inclusive Leader assessment. She was instrumental in the push to create a scalable platform for the assessment to increase its reach beyond just the top executives and expand into middle management. Alina grew up in Siberia and immigrated to Canada at a young age. She is married to a Brazilian man.

The 5 Disciplines of Inclusive Organizations coauthor, Fayruz Kirtzman, is Korn Ferry's Global DE&I Diagnostic Solutions Leader. Along with Senior Principal Gustavo Gisbert, Fayruz and I were the originators of the groundbreaking Korn Ferry DE&I Maturity model. The 5 Disciplines of Inclusive Organizations are an outgrowth of that work. Fayruz is of Arabic descent, grew up in Germany in a German household, and later moved to New York City where she and her husband, who is of Jewish descent, are raising their children.

The coauthor for this book, *The 5 Disciplines of Inclusive Teams*, Michel Buffet, is one of Korn Ferry's leading Top Teams executive coaches. We first partnered to steer an interdisciplinary internal Korn Ferry team to refine, test, and launch the inclusive teams model and skill-building learning modules. In this third and final book of the trilogy, we sought to codify the disciplines inclusive teams use to achieve breakthrough collaboration, innovation, and business outcomes. Empirical research shows the undeniable correlation between more diverse and inclusive teams and greater innovation and effectiveness. In this book we crack the code of how and why. Michel has Spanish and French heritage and lives in the United States with his husband and children.

It was over five years ago that I first thought of applying the 5 Disciplines rubric to self, organization, and team. This book brings full circle the narrative arc and compelling business case that diversity, practiced inclusively, yields results far greater than a solo voice could—and allows teams to become far more than the simple sum of their parts.

$$1 + 1 = X^{x:}$$

Andrés T. Tapia

INTRODUCTION

Diverse and Inclusive Teams Transform the Future

OR SEVENTEEN DAYS NO ONE KNEW IF the miners were alive. Thirty-three men were trapped seven hundred meters underground and five kilometers from the entrance of the San José copper and gold mine near the town of Copiapó in the Atacama Desert of Chile. But then, on August 22, 2010, a note was found taped to a drill bit that had been probing for signs of life as it was pulled back to the surface:

"Estamos bien en el refugio los 33."
("We are well in the shelter, the 33 of us.")

Next, one of history's most complex and dangerous rescue operations went into high gear. Teams of scientists and engineers from NASA and a dozen global corporations from various Latin American countries, South Africa, Australia, the United States, and Canada joined excavators from three drilling rig teams and specialists from nearly every ministry of the Chilean government to work around the clock to save the miners. Drills broke, equipment with too much weight threatened cave-ins, and there were mounting worries about keeping the miners alive as their health deteriorated.

Sixty-nine days later, the men were brought to the surface one at a time in a specially built capsule, with over 5 million people around the world watching via video stream.

It took a team. A diverse and inclusive team.

. . .

During the Covid-19 pandemic, the spirits company Beam Suntory was focused on keeping up the spirits of people worldwide with its top-shelf gins and whiskies. But supply chain disruptions and the company's organizational departments, siloed by geography and internal reward systems, were leading to the hoarding of product and an uneven distribution around the world.

CEO Albert Baladi quickly identified the structural barriers to team collaboration. He mobilized executive management to break the long-standing reward system that had disincentivized global collaboration.

"We are going to sink or swim together," he said as he challenged his various teams around the world.

A new, collective team-oriented approach held together by one global sales metric opened the floodgates of creative, organization-wide collaboration. Product began to be diverted in globally crisscrossing ways to meet the high demand for take-out *quarantinis* among an angst-ridden world in domestic lockdown.

It took a team. A diverse, inclusive, and incentivized team.

■ ■ ■

Korn Ferry employees from Russia, the United States, India, and Perú had less than three days to design and deliver a highly interactive session for a music festival promotion client. The idea involved generating innovative high-engagement experiences for Gen Z fans at an upcoming Latino music festival. The team had a "minimal viable product" tool kit but no content for this very specific ask.

In the "let's dive in" agile response, a key human insight was that there was no such thing as a prototypical Latino Gen Z persona that could be designed for. Instead, there were dozens of Latino Gen Z personas due to the hyper-intersectionality of identities under the big umbrella of "Latino." It was a great insight, but there was no time to generate all those personas in the race against the clock to deliver for the session.

This is when the team brought in another member—ChatGPT. In rapid prompt-and-response sessions between the team members with the knowledge of what intersectionality can look like and the artificial intelligence (AI) platform's ability to quickly turn that knowledge into first-person testimonials, the team was able to generate nearly twenty different personas reflecting a rich spectrum of Latino diversity. On the day of the session the team was ready with a breakthrough experience that generated differentiated and valuable insight the client could rapidly put to work.

It took a team. A diverse, inclusive, and AI-powered team.

WHY THE FOCUS ON TEAMS?

In all of these stories, it took a diverse team acting inclusively to get out of the metaphorical escape room. They illustrate how diverse and inclusive teams working toward a shared purpose can develop breakthrough solutions to address a wide range of needs.

We live in an age moving at warp speed. Nearly every area of our lives and society has a different way of working than, let's say, *yesterday.* Just look at the speed of technological adoption in most of our lifetimes. For 50 million people to adopt computers, mobile phones, the internet, and Facebook it took fourteen, twelve, seven, and three years, respectively. And then, between November 2022 and January 2023—a mere two months—100 million were using ChatGPT (see figure 1).[1]

At this speed of change, traditional ways of organizing enterprises are not delivering what the market needs. Rigid silos are getting in the way and bureaucracy is choking the flow of collaboration and innovation.

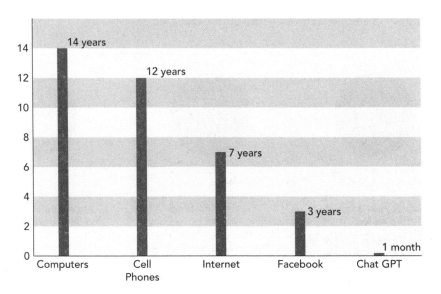

Figure 1: How long it took each technology to reach 50 million users (Adapted by and used by permission of Korn Ferry from visualcapitalist.com/how -long-does-it-take-to-hit-50-million-users)

Moreover, in-person face-to-face interaction is becoming less of a practical reality. With all these challenges, research shows that teams are losing more than twenty hours per month due to unclear communication and collaboration.[2] The old norms are obsolete (figure 2), and new ones must be established.

To respond to the minute-by-minute barrage of challenges, opportunities, and new knowledge, we need agility more than we need new standard operating procedures. Agile financial services organizations are two times more likely to attain top-quartile financial results compared to those that have average organizational agility, according to a study based on Accenture's Organizational Agility Index.[3] Additionally, 92 percent of C-suites say organizational agility is critical for the future.[4]

What is the key to this agility? For sure, it involves systems and processes that are easy to use by everyone. But who creates those systems and processes? Teams. Teams have been the basic organizational unit since the dawn of time—as in early humans going on group hunts for mastodons—but today, in this digital, post-pandemic era, something transformational is happening.

Before going further, let's pause and define what a team is, because a group of people working independently doesn't make a team—just like a bunch of components of a watch don't *make* a watch.

Silos are in the way; hierarchy is flatter.

Face-to-face is less of a reality.

Teams are losing *20+* hours per month due to unclear collaboration and communication.

Agility, fluidity, spontaneity are needed more than structures, processes, and in-person meetings.

92% of C-suite executives say agility is critical for the future.

Agile organizations are twice as likely to attain top financial results.

Organizations consider teams—not practices, lines of business, nor offices—the key organizing principle in which to get work done.

Teams are *50%* more efficient at completing tasks than individuals.

Figure 2: The organizational ways of organizing enterprises are not working anymore (Korn Ferry, 2023)

At its essence, a team is *a small group of people who are working toward a common purpose and performance goal with an agreed-on working approach and complementary skills, and who hold each other accountable.*

As the smallest organizational units within enterprises, teams—not practices, nor lines of business, nor offices—are the organizing principle through which work gets done. In fact, teams are 50 percent more efficient at completing tasks than individuals.[5]

Teams are also the fulcrum on which organizations pivot to meet the challenges of the relentless pace of change. Teams are the ultimate morphing entity. They are autonomous and adaptable. They can come together, break apart, and then reconfigure, with members belonging to multiple teams at a time. They can be of various sizes, exist for any length, and accommodate any person, anywhere. To be an effective team requires mutual consultation, coordinated action, and shared decision-making—that is, collaboration.

Collaboration is the vital currency of teams in an era in which collaboration is more vital than ever. Salesforce reports that 86 percent of executives cite ineffective collaboration as a major contributor to business failures.[6] The CEO of Barilla, Gianluca Di Tondo, declared early in his tenure (which started in 2023) that his priority would be to push decisions down to the manager and team level, which he sees as essential for creating a sustainable future—a huge change for the hierarchical 140-year-old company.[7] And the CEO of Yum! Brands, David Gibbs, has declared collaboration a critical priority and a key to innovation across the company's iconic restaurant brands—Pizza Hut, KFC, Taco Bell, and The Habit Burger Grill.[8]

One CEO has already gone into hyperdrive in this direction. In March 2024 Bayer CEO Bill Anderson eliminated thousands of managerial roles and traditional business divisions. He unleashed his global staff of one hundred thousand to form five thousand to six thousand self-directed teams to increase employee initiatives, product ideas, and time-to-market speed in the next few years.[9] In his anti-bureaucracy and pro-agile teams manifesto published in *Fortune*, Anderson stated,

> At Bayer, we have begun a massive effort to redesign every job and every process, with a radical focus on customers and products. Most importantly, we're putting 95% of decision-making in the hands of the people actually doing

> the work. This means many fewer managers and layers, and replacing hierarchical annual budgets with 90-day sprints by self-directed teams. . . . This model, which we've coined Dynamic Shared Ownership . . . [will mean that] rather than a lumbering corporation, Bayer will emerge as agile and bold as a startup—but one with operations in more than 100 countries. I'm convinced that this dramatic change will accelerate and unlock the value creation in each of our businesses.[10]

Collaborative teams help each other find accurate information so they can free up more time to work on useful solutions. (The average knowledge employee spends roughly 2.5 hours a day gathering information.[11]) In collaborative teams, employees learn from one another due to the multiple inputs from diverse points of view and experiences. This improves problem-solving capabilities and creative thinking, increasing the organization's ability to adapt in a changing market environment. This, in turn, creates an engaged workforce in which each person feels like a contributing member of a unified team.

Not only is this collaboration engaging, but it's also measurably more productive. A Stanford study found that those who work in a collaborative rather than an individual setting are 50 percent more effective at completing tasks, which boosts their intrinsic motivation and helps them become more engaged with their work.[12]

TODAY'S MOST EFFECTIVE TEAMS ARE DIVERSE AND INCLUSIVE

Teams have become the way in which people navigate the intricate structures of Big Business or Big Government and get things done. As Anderson, Bayer's CEO, wrote:

> There's another sinister force weighing on the company's strategic options. Bureaucracy has put Bayer in a stranglehold. Our internal rules for employees span 1,362 pages. We have excellent people, with expertise in a range of disciplines and exceptional commitment to our success. But they are trapped in 12 levels of hierarchy, which puts

unnecessary distance between our teams, our customers, and our products. . . . To succeed, we need an environment where people and their ideas can thrive—not be stymied by red tape.[13]

Given our research and practice, we would add that for this ambition to succeed, CEOs must consider the reality of the vast diversity that exists at the team level. Today's workforce is diverse in every imaginable way—race and ethnicity, gender, physical ability, and sexual orientation, yes, but also in differentiated ways that are tied to our personalities (introvert versus extrovert), thinking styles (neurodivergence), and unique life experiences. The bell curve of diversity in the workplace currently lies at the entry- and mid-level jobs—the very place where teams are at their most numerous and active.

The full spectrum of diversity comes to life and delivers concrete and measurable outcomes in the context of teams. So, to discuss today's teams, we *must* discuss diverse teams. How can diversity be more than just a characteristic but an enabler of teams performing at their best? The key to leveraging that diversity is to nurture and shape *inclusive* teams.

Teams are where employees have the greatest chance to feel they belong, can bring their full selves to work, and can do their best work. These are the conditions that teams require to collaborate effectively, to be agile, and to rise to the challenge of self-direction that delivers innovation and optimized results (figure 3).

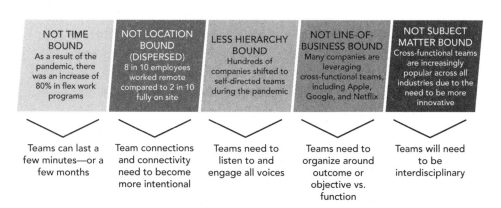

Figure 3: The nature of teams is changing (Korn Ferry, 2023)

INNOVATION IS A TEAM SPORT

In a world of disruption, 80 percent of global companies have declared innovation to be one of their top three priorities.[14] Innovation leads to new products and services and improves processes and structures. It leads to expansion into new markets, including more diverse ones. It fuels a sense of progress and accomplishment that plays a big part in driving engagement. This clarion call is why innovation receives focused attention in this book.

Contrary to its portrayal in popular culture, research shows that innovation is a team sport. And it is diverse, inclusive teams that create the conditions for greater innovation. While teams make better decisions than individuals 66 percent of the time, diverse teams make better decisions 87 percent of the time.[15] However, maximizing the power of diversity to achieve breakthrough collaboration and innovation across global geographies has remained out of reach. That's because it's not just the diversity of the teams that leads to greater innovation—it's their inclusiveness. Diversity alone is not enough. You can't just put a diverse team together and expect to see the documented benefits sprout organically. In fact, when not managed well, diverse teams can end up being more conflictual and less productive.[16] Left alone, they are likely to perform worse than a more homogenous team because the greater the number of differences there are in a team, the greater the potential for conflict.

To optimize that diversity and, in fact, to be able to navigate the greater complexity and enhanced possibility of friction inherent in diverse teams, teams must be inclusive. A Boston Consulting Group (BCG) study analyzing more than 1,700 companies worldwide found that inclusive teams were more innovative, producing 45 percent of a company's total revenue from innovation compared to only 26 percent from non-inclusive teams.[17] Diverse and inclusive teams have an increased potential for innovation when the sparks from the greater friction are effectively nurtured. When that is done, these sparks can ignite the fire of unexpected breakthroughs.

As you can see, diverse *and* inclusive teams are the winning combination for innovation. In other words:

**Top team performance and innovation are the *so-what*
of diversity and inclusion.**

Teams are where innovation and better business results come to life. It's where the energy for shaping the future is stored and ready to be activated. And it's diversity and inclusion that increases the octane of team innovation, business results, and activation.

WHY WE WROTE THIS BOOK

The higher potential of diverse and inclusive teams is too great to leave to chance. It requires the deliberate activation of inclusion for the diversity within teams to thrive. Hence, we set out to crack the code of how to unlock the collective power of diverse teams through inclusion.

Here's how we came together.

This is the third book in the Five Inclusive Disciplines trilogy, which explores how we can harness the dynamic power of inclusive leaders (book 1), organizations (book 2), and teams (book 3). As Andrés wrote in the prologue, he intentionally worked with different coauthors for each book—not only to walk the talk of diversity and inclusion, but to reap its profound benefits. Each of these books is infinitely better for the diversity of thought, experience, and expertise of their coauthors.

Andrés is Korn Ferry's Global Diversity and Inclusion Strategist. Michel is Korn Ferry's Top Team Performance Solution Leader. We first partnered to steer an interdisciplinary internal Korn Ferry team to refine, test, and launch the inclusive teams model and skill-building learning modules. Our very different backgrounds and the dynamic collaboration they sparked made it a no-brainer to work together on a book based on our inclusive teams model. Of course, we also had some powerful shared goals.

For both of us, with a collective four decades of consulting experience in organizations of profound influence in the economy and in the world, it's about crystalizing and capturing key learnings to be able to share them with as many leaders and practitioners as possible. We also see the need for more diverse teams that reflect our societies. For sure, it's the right thing to do from a social justice and human rights perspective. But it's also the right thing to do from the vantage point of talent optimization, innovation, business outcomes, and shaping a more creative, healthier, and sustainable future.

There is so much research that supports the idea that more diverse teams drive greater performance and innovation. Now, more understanding is needed about *how* inclusion and diversity drive performance and innovation. Our intent was to observe and codify what inclusive teams do to effectively optimize their diversity.

At Korn Ferry, we set out to find the behaviors and practices in which high-performing, diverse, and inclusive teams were engaging. Once identified, we explored ways to codify those practices and accelerate the process of leveraging team diversity through inclusion.

We took an agile, interdisciplinary approach. Rather than seeking an airtight model based on years of research, we brought in the best and latest research from a variety of disciplines—neuroscience, psychology, and cross-cultural communication, as well as from The Korn Ferry Institute's (KFI) research on inclusive leadership and inclusive organizations (as presented in the first two books in the Five Inclusive Disciplines trilogy).

We also plumbed KFI research on how highly effective teams that did not consider diversity and inclusion achieved success. We then engaged our global DE&I consultants on what it would take for these teams to be inclusive and, from there, how they could achieve even better business outcomes.

We tested various hypotheses through thousands of consulting engagements and research investigations with the KFI and academics such as our adviser, Dr. Anita Woolley. We also cross-correlated our own previous research findings on inclusive leaders and inclusive organizations.

One intriguing dimension we want to highlight is the neuroscience research we found on teams. The new proof points coming out of neuroscience show that when people exhibit inclusive behaviors like checking their unconscious biases, being curious, showing empathy, and trusting, it releases mood-enhancing hormones within a group. For example, oxytocin—which accelerates social bonding—releases in inverse proportionality to the stress hormone cortisol. (Yes, the one that causes anxiety, depression, fatigue, and irritability.)

What does that mean? What was once a pejorative dismissal—that discriminatory treatment is "all in your head"—can now be affirmed as objectively true!

It also means that now that we know this cause and effect, we can design interventions that can generate the types of mindsets and behaviors that release more oxytocin, which becomes a vital enhancer of inclusion, which in turn leads to a better-performing team.

"Neuroscience represents a new frontier in our increased ability to leverage data from physical science in addition to social science in support of existing theories as well as in the development of new practices," says Amelia Haynes, Korn Ferry neuroscientist.[18]

Along the way we used these different research methodologies:

- Qualitative: primary and secondary research case studies on the connection between inclusive leaders, inclusive teams, innovation, and team results
- Quantitative: KFI work on effective teams

Which brings us to our findings: the 5 Disciplines of Inclusive Teams.

Our research on teams drills down on what effective inclusive and diverse teams look like, how they operate, and how they optimize their performance—including achieving the promise that more diverse and inclusive organizations are more innovative and are better able to achieve organizational results (figure 4).

Figure 4: The Inclusive Teams Model (Korn Ferry, 2023)

DISCIPLINE 1—CONNECTING *TO BUILD AFFILIATION*

The ability to deeply understand and value the capabilities, professional experiences, and identity-forming biography of each team member.

Teams simply don't spend enough time or intention connecting with the fullness of team members' skill sets. Through Connecting, team members lay the foundation for all their collaborative work.

DISCIPLINE 2—CARING *TO NURTURE PSYCHOLOGICAL SAFETY*

The ability of team members to demonstrate personal concern for one another as well as for the team as an entity.

Caring is the ability of team members to be curious about the personal side of their teammates and empathize with their life situations. A team where people feel they are seen and valued for who they are will be more cohesive, collaborative, and innovative.

DISCIPLINE 3—SYNCHRONIZING *TO HARNESS COLLECTIVE INTELLIGENCE*

The state of being coordinated in time and purpose, where multiple elements or entities align collaboratively and harmoniously through systems, networks, and devices.

Call it chemistry, flow, intangibles, or secret sauce. Neuroscientists call it synchrony. It's what taps and harnesses the collective intelligence of teams—and it can be activated by team interactions that respectfully tap into people's sense of identity.[19]

DISCIPLINE 4—CULTURAL DEXTERITY *TO INTEGRATE DIVERSE PERSPECTIVES*

The ability of team members to discern and consider their own and others' worldviews, solve problems, make decisions, and resolve conflicts in ways that optimize cultural differences for better, longer-lasting, and more creative solutions.

Today's inclusive teams are skilled at navigating all forms of differences by mastering the practices of being self-aware and culturally curious, and of developing ways to leverage those differences as a team with its own unique identity.

DISCIPLINE 5—POWERSHARING *TO ENSURE EQUITABLE CONTRIBUTIONS*

The ability to unlock the power of each team member equitably to yield the best and most creative results.

In inclusive teams power is shared across all team members. Power—to move things forward, to influence, to inform, to create—flows as a surge of electricity in the neural network of the team's collective intelligence. *Who* has the power ebbs and flows among the team members based on the topic, task, or mood and considers who has the contextually relevant expertise and knowledge that inherently gives them authority to contribute with power.

The 5 Disciplines are a collection of inclusive team practices and behaviors that we hope become the default for all teams. The upshot of the first two disciplines, Connecting and Caring, is that trust deepens, and, with that, nurtures an environment where team members can feel psychologically safe. This allows team members to take more risks with one another, which is key to the practice of the disciplines of Synchronizing, Cultural Dexterity, and Powersharing. This is why Connecting and Caring are represented as the outer circle in our model.

PARADOXES OF INCLUSIVE TEAMS

At every turn in our research, we came across paradoxes of inclusive teams that demand attention. For all the positives that can come from skilled and committed execution of the practices within each of the disciplines, teams can overdo any one of them.

Too much Connecting can create separatist cliques. Too much Caring can lead to low accountability. Too much Synchronizing contributes to groupthink. Too much Cultural Dexterity can foster moral relativism. Too much Powersharing can lead to anarchy.

Too much of a good thing is good for nothing, as the saying goes. We acknowledge this up front to give us license to write with the optimism and confidence these disciplines deserve.

One additional paradox to note is on the role of the leader in increasingly self-empowered teams.

As we describe the increased autonomy with which inclusive teams can operate—due to organizations' increasing need for agile decision-making as well as the vast collective intelligence of high-performing diverse and inclusive teams—you might be wondering: What is the role of the team leader? Is there still a need for one?

We think yes, but not in the traditional way. We will also need to establish new norms around the role of the leader. There is a spectrum of options for how this can play out, from teams with fully directive leaders to teams with leaders as player-coaches and process facilitators to truly autonomous teams. The bottom line, however, is that inclusive leaders are needed to facilitate teams in practicing and embodying the 5 Disciplines of Inclusive Teams.

We have already dedicated one full book in this trilogy to the leader's role, so we are not going to write much from the leader's perspective. While the majority of this book is written from the perspective of the team, we do provide our vision for the future of leadership as well as a guide for team members and team leaders on charting a path to an inclusive team.

HOW THIS BOOK IS ORGANIZED

Part 1 is an exploration of the 5 Disciplines: the research, the stories, and the "how" of living out each discipline for optimal impact. We provide the key practices (the behaviors shaped by mindsets, routines, and techniques) for each discipline that become the habits of inclusive teams. At the end of part 1, we discuss the paradoxes associated with each discipline and how they interact with each other to create a holistic practice of inclusion.

Throughout, we stay grounded in key findings in neuroscience to back up our assertions and recommendations. These are illustrated through the Neuroscience Corner feature by our colleague, KFI neuroscience expert Amelia Haynes.

Readers will also come across additional insightful contributions in the form of topical or first-person sidebars by a diverse pool of contributors whom we admire and work with at Korn Ferry.

In **part 2** we look forward to our exciting vision for inclusive teams in the world of work, and the breakthroughs we believe they can achieve in the areas of innovation and leadership and in creating a new, sustainable business-grounded direction for DE&I.

We have all been part of a team at work, school, in a sport, musical group, or a spiritual community—there are an infinite number of contexts. Most of us have experienced being on dysfunctional teams or so-so teams, as well as ones we wish could last forever.

Today the default is the so-so team.

This book is about shifting the default. It's about how to be a part of an excellent, inclusive, hugely productive, and invigorating team—the type we wish could last forever.

We believe we have cracked the code for any group of people to quickly come together and do great things for the benefit of each individual in the group, the team itself, their organizations, and even society at large.

Together, let's unlock the collective power of teams. Let's achieve breakthrough!

THE 5 DISCIPLINES OF INCLUSIVE TEAMS

Let's dive into the 5 Disciplines and the many practices—tactical, mindset, and strategic—required to create a high-collaboration, high-innovation, and high-performance environment.

The first two disciplines—*Connecting* and *Caring*—are like two halves of a circle, encircling and embracing the entirety of the approach.

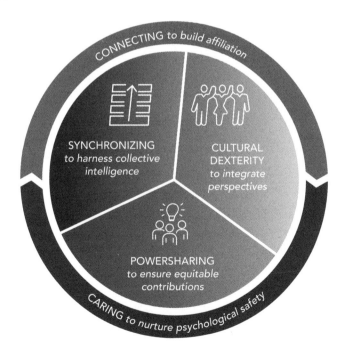

Figure 4: The Inclusive Teams Model (Korn Ferry, 2023)

Everything begins with these two—they lay the groundwork for the other three disciplines. In other words, *Cultural Dexterity*, *Synchronizing*, and *Powersharing* reach their fullest potential in the trusting, empathetic, and supportive environment created when team members engage in Connecting and Caring.

In part 1 of this book, you will gain a deep and practical understanding of how your teams can employ the 5 Disciplines—individually, combined, and in just the right measure—to unlock their collective power and achieve break-through.

* * *

1

Discipline 1: *Connecting* to Build Affiliation

A dream you dream alone is only a dream.
A dream you dream together is reality.

—*Yoko Ono, Japanese multimedia*
artist, songwriter, and peace activist

EVEN WITH THE COVID-19 PANDEMIC IN THE RECENT past for most, many are still reluctant to fully enter physical communal spaces, and they remain tethered to screens. Fears about safety while commuting for people from non-majority populations (based on race, sex, sexual orientation, and gender, for example) are well grounded. So is, for those in the United States, the anxiety around finding oneself trapped in another random mass shooting. So are, for people everywhere, concerns about adding to the planet's carbon footprint through commuting.

CONNECTING

The ability to deeply understand and value the capabilities, professional experiences, and identity-forming biography of each team member.

Connecting remains a challenge even for the growing number of workers returning to the office in full- or part-time capacities, especially for the millions who began new jobs during the pandemic, and not to mention the generation who began their professional careers in physical isolation.

More than half of US adults (58 percent) are experiencing loneliness, according to a recent study by the Cigna Group, with people from underrepresented racial groups experiencing loneliness at higher rates.[1] For example, 75 percent of Hispanic adults and 68 percent of Black/African American adults are classified as lonely—10 points higher than the rate for the total adult population.[2] Fueled in part by this mass loneliness, 42 percent of Americans are reporting symptoms of anxiety and depression.[3]

It's worse in the workplace: 72 percent of employees report feeling lonely at least once a month and 70 percent of employees who now work remotely feel lonelier than before they made the switch.[4] In its 2023 Belonging Barometer 2.0 study, EY found that more than 80 percent of employee respondents globally from one specific company have felt or feel lonely at work, with 49 percent feeling lonelier than they did prior to the pandemic. Stunningly, 90 percent of employees suffering from loneliness said they would not tell their supervisor they were struggling.[5]

This epidemic of loneliness has a significant bottom line financial impact. Employee disconnection is one of the main drivers of voluntary turnover, "with lonely employees costing U.S. companies up to $406 billion a year," according to the *Harvard Business Review*.[6] Conversely, BetterUp found that employees who experience high levels of belonging have decreased turnover risk, increased job performance, a reduction in sick days, and an increased employer promoter score, which results in annual savings of $52 million for a ten-thousand-person company. Teams that score in the top 20 percent in relational engagement realize a 41 percent reduction in absenteeism and 59 percent less turnover.[7]

The antidote to this mass isolation and loneliness is clearly **Connecting**, our first discipline of inclusive teams. As primal—and some may say obvious—as this need is for us, we're failing at it, especially in our work teams. In BetterUp's 2022 *The Connection Crisis Report*, 69 percent of employees surveyed said they aren't satisfied with the opportunities for connection at work.[8] And while most human resources (HR) professionals (85 percent)—who arguably specialize in employee well-being—agree that connection between employees in the workforce is critical, just 31 percent of HR respondents say they've adequately addressed the challenges with employee connection at work.[9]

We need to revisit how to effectively connect in this new post-Covid age, including addressing the generational divides that Covid and remote work have put into starker contrast. And we better figure this out quickly because the effect of not connecting is devastating to work productivity and innovation as well as emotional health.

CONNECTING WITHIN INCLUSIVE TEAMS

Connecting with others is an evolved trait. Humans began living in groups as a mechanism to support cooperative behaviors like hunting and grooming. Today, relationships with others are a kind of cooperative behavior that offers the support critical to navigating a competitive world.

Twentieth-century thinker Abraham Maslow posited that connecting with others is essential to meeting all of our human needs—from the most basic, such as survival (e.g., group hunts that made sure there was enough food for the tribe and GoFundMe projects for critical medical treatments), to the higher-end ones, such as self-actualization (e.g., friends and family coming together to celebrate a graduation and teams galvanizing to develop a cure for Huntington's disease). But connection also has benefits that lie below the surface. For example, humans release more endorphins and more oxytocin—two neurotransmitters involved in reward processing in the brain—when we interact with friends. In other words, the act of connecting is its own reward.

NEUROSCIENCE CORNER

Connecting Boosts Health

Amelia Haynes

The effects of having close personal connections at work are much more profound than simply having a buddy to talk to during the week. Connecting with others plays a significant role in our psychological, physical, and organizational health. This may be because deep personal connections make us feel safe. In fact, these kinds of connections measurably decrease our biological stress responses. Studies show that when we are in the presence of a friend, we release less cortisol when we experience something unpleasant compared to when we are alone. The presence of someone we feel connected to modulates the production of stress hormones in our bodies.

These findings have led to the hypothesis that one of the primary functions of friendship, from an evolutionary perspective, is stress reduction. Deep personal connections can help us cope with a difficult work issue, making our experience of it more positive. The result? In environments that support deep connections, people are not only happier, but they are also more likely to speak up and have candid conversations, and they are less likely to second-guess their colleagues.

Not surprisingly, then, organizations that foster connection have higher customer satisfaction, fewer safety incidents, and overall higher profit margins. In fact, there is a direct link from connection to engagement to business results, according to Gallup. The analytics and advisory company uses connection-related data, such as having a best friend at work or feeling your boss cares about you as a person, to measure engagement, and reports that highly engaged business unit teams result in a 23 percent difference in profitability.[10]

In the workplace—whether physical or virtual—where so many of us spend a substantial portion of our time, the most likely avenue for connection is within teams. They are the platform not only for getting work done but also for social connection and supportive relationships. At least, they can be. Even in this smallest unit of organizational culture, connection does not happen automatically. Sometimes, it can feel even more isolating and lonely to be the "only one" on a team than it is to work alone.

Connecting within an inclusive team goes way deeper than team members just sharing their title and tenure in the organization. This says so little about each team member's full range of capabilities and experiences. Rather, it's about forging strong professional team bonds that will result in enhanced team performance.

Please note the emphasis here on getting to know the professional and intellectual qualities of the team members versus getting to know them more personally. In the Inclusive Teams model, we reserve the practices and dynamics of the more personal nature to the second discipline of Caring, which we will explore in the next chapter.

The first and foundational inclusive team discipline of Connecting leads to team members of all backgrounds and abilities feeling valued for their skills, training, and experience. The result is greater physical, mental, and emotional health, increased engagement, and better business outcomes.[11, 12, 13]

Let's look at three key Connecting practices that inclusive teams do well:

- Exhibiting Curiosity
- Building Trust
- Sharing a Common Purpose

EXHIBITING CURIOSITY

Members of inclusive teams express curiosity about what each person brings to the team in terms of their formal and informal credentials, skill sets, and work experiences. By nurturing this curiosity, they gain a better understanding of their peers' perspectives, interests, strengths, and motivations, and their peers feel more comfortable revealing more of themselves and what they can offer to the team.

Individuals with perfunctory interest versus genuine curiosity often engage their team members in rote, noncreative, and nonpersonal ways. For example, they may see and interact with people befitting their position or tenure without digging deeper to learn who the person behind the title is. On the other hand, inclusive team members practice curiosity through active listening and asking open-ended questions about people's specific educational, work, and life experiences. When curiosity is reciprocated among team members, connection increases—and with it, knowledge of people's capabilities that could move the needle on team performance.

Curiosity about others is what led Bill Gates and Steve Jobs to team up. Though they initially were pitted against one another as fierce competitors in the technology industry, their shared interest in innovation and curiosity about each other led to a series of exciting conversations and strategic collaborations, as detailed by journalist Malcolm Gladwell in his bestseller *Outliers*.[14]

As Gladwell noted, "The more Jobs came to know about Gates, the more impressed he was. 'He's actually a really good guy,' Jobs said." This shift in perception was driven by Jobs's curiosity about Gates's motivations and ideas. And this curiosity-driven connection led to the joint development of new technologies, such as the Microsoft Office Suite for Macintosh computers, and paved the way for greater cooperation and communication within the tech industry.

THE THREE QUESTIONS

How can we show curiosity for what people bring to the team without being uncomfortably intrusive? We have developed a surefire way we call *The Three Questions*. Team leaders can ask these questions one on one or in a group. They can also encourage team members to initiate *Three Questions* conversations among themselves.

This approach starts with a preface to appropriately frame what is happening. Here's how it goes.

1. Provide context.

    I was reading this book on inclusive teams and it encouraged team members to ask each other about how we can best work together.

2. Ask for consent.

    Would you be interested in a conversation to learn more about each other in that way? If not, no worries.

3. Reciprocate.

    And if we do have that conversation, I would be happy to share about myself as well.

In our work, we have found that most people approached this way are open to sharing about their professional selves. Why? Because many people like being asked about themselves, especially things they wish their colleagues knew about them so their skills could be leveraged more effectively. It is stunning how little people tend to know about the breadth and depth of their teammates' skills and experiences, much less how they can be leveraged for greater team impact.

And now, The Three Questions:

1. In our work together, what's one thing about you that I don't know, that you would like me to know?

2. If you were to bring more of that skill/experience/mindset to work, what would that look like and what do you believe the impact would be?

3. What would you need from me as your teammate [or manager] to be able to do that?

When team members have these types of *Three Questions* conversations with each other on a regular basis, it strengthens their connections. Showing this type of professional curiosity is a powerful connector because it makes people feel seen and valued for what they bring to the workplace. It is also a powerful performance enhancer because it leads to team members being tapped more effectively for their contributions.

BUILDING TRUST

Trust in one's coworkers is associated with greater organizational commitment, increased job satisfaction, greater attraction to the organization, and lower employee turnover. Individuals rated high on trust (i.e., they are trusting) tend to give others the benefit of the doubt even when mistakes happen. Their connections are strong and resilient. Additionally, knowing that you are trusted generates greater feelings of well-being and greater connection. In this way, trust creates a virtuous cycle of positivity that benefits individuals and the whole team.

Inclusive teams trust that each member will get their work done. They make trust building a priority and do all they can to address areas of distrust related to team accountabilities and goals. The more each individual trusts their teammates to get the work done, the lower the tendency to micromanage.[15] This leads to increased autonomy, lower job insecurity, and greater "meaningfulness" of work, all of which deepen trust and team connectivity.[16] And when everyone feels connected and can trust each other to stick to their word and follow through on their commitments, the more good work can be done. KFI research confirms that teams with greater trust and collaboration achieve more. They make better decisions and deliver better financial results.[17]

There are many reasons, often justified, for team members to not trust each other, some of which may have little or nothing to do with the team itself. For example, conflicts within a team due to interpersonal relationship dynamics (related or not to the team's work) are common. Teams may also contain members from a diversity of backgrounds, some of whom have experienced racism, homophobia, ableism, ageism, or other forms of discrimination. As such, they may be wary of trusting members of groups that may have hurt them in the past or they may be particularly sensitive to acts of unconscious bias even by well-intentioned team members.

Addressing these complex dynamics often requires outside help in the form of individual therapy, mediation, and professional consequences for misconduct. There are many well-researched and elaborate best practices for these different types of interventions that we won't try to do justice to here, except to say individual team members must be open to exploring their own reasons for lack of trust when they go beyond the scope of a work team and the manager. Part of this exploration should include an acknowledgment of our human tendency to more easily trust people who are like us or whom we have known longer.

At one of our clients in the pharmaceutical industry there was a team leader who needed to assign a new project to a team member. He had two people in mind, Margarita and Laurent, who both had the necessary skills and expertise. Margarita was someone the manager had worked with closely for several years and he knew her well. Laurent was new to the team, and while he had a good track record, the leader didn't know him as well.

Given his closer relationship with Margarita, the leader felt more comfortable assigning the project to her. While both Margarita and Laurent's credibility and reliability were important, the emotional connection and trust the manager had built up over time played an *inequitable* role in his decision-making process. So, the manager defaulted to the person he knew best and who was more like him. But to tap into the full potential of a diverse team, inclusive leaders must be careful to not have overreliance on the comfort they feel with some team members over others.

It's understandable that managers may be reluctant to give assignments to people they don't know as well, but this only proves why connection is so important. In such circumstances, practicing curiosity and getting to know the full dimension of each team member's skills, education, and experiences would go far to build trust and lead to more equitable decision-making. Inclusive teams don't leave anyone behind.

SHARING A COMMON PURPOSE

The 1995 Rugby World Cup was hosted by South Africa. At the time, the nation was undergoing a significant transition from apartheid to becoming a democratic society. The South African rugby team, the Springboks, represented a nation cleaved along racial and cultural lines. There was one Black player on the team and, historically, a Black person wearing the Springboks jersey was considered an affront to Whites.

Team captain Francois Pienaar, with guidance from President Nelson Mandela, inspired the Springboks to find a shared purpose not just for themselves but for the country, bringing unity and reconciliation to a racially divided nation.

But before striving for such a lofty purpose, the Springboks had a more immediate goal: winning the rugby tournament. This more attainable shared objective galvanized the team; as a collective, they were playing for all of South Africa. With this important goal within their reach, the Springboks went on to win the Rugby World Cup.

Their shared win led to the entire nation celebrating together—previously unthinkable given the systemic separation of the races under apartheid. It brought the country one step closer to the ideal of racial reconciliation and national unity. Post-celebration surveys reflected a more optimistic view of the country's future. As a result, initiatives were

---

PARADOX: CONNECTING CAN LEAD TO EXCLUSIONARY CLIQUES!

Learn more in chapter 6.

■

---

launched to promote rugby and other sports in historically overlooked communities as a means of integrating different racial groups.

Few things focus a team to work collaboratively and inclusively like shared purpose. The KFI's research on traits and competencies shows that the trait of *affiliation* (which is one way to connect to others who have a common purpose) is linked to positive business outcomes.[18] In fact, shared purpose is, to mix metaphors, both the glue that keeps a team together and the propellent to get things done.

As the Springboks' story shows, having shared purpose is also the most effective practice to soften the edges of differences of all kinds. It is the bigger picture that allows team members to recognize how their individual roles—and others'—contribute to the larger goals of the group. We are all more motivated to work together and harder when we can identify each person's part in achieving a common goal.

While the work of creating a shared purpose falls on team leaders initially, members of inclusive teams play a critical role in identifying how individual goals might come together to achieve that shared purpose. It often starts with a growth mindset that embraces challenges, persistence in the face of setbacks, and seeing possibilities where others may see limitations.

PULLING IT ALL TOGETHER

There was an executive at a prestigious nonprofit who was known for being exceptionally competent at his job—smart, focused, efficient—but his team's results, while positive, were not transformational.

In assessing if he was leading his team inclusively, it became evident that while he had a gentle way about him, he came across as aloof and unknowable when relating to his team members.

In a coaching session to get to the heart of the matter, he was asked how well he knew his team members and vice versa.

"Not very much at all," he answered. "I know them for their skills and credentials, but I have no idea about the reality of their work and the life experiences that may have shaped how they approach their work."

While he admitted it would be nice to know more about his people, and to share his own compelling background and experiences, he claimed there was no time.

His coach suggested he try connecting more with his team as an experiment. They asked him to find opportunities to ask his people about who they are within the context of work.

A few weeks later, the executive reported back enthusiastically on the results of the experiment. He had used a variation of The Three Questions with four new employees at an onboarding dinner. Usually, he used these dinners to discuss the dos and don'ts for succeeding in their complex organization. This time, he started the conversation with The Three Questions. He asked them about their origin stories and their motivation for joining the organization. Important information about how they could uniquely contribute to the mission poured out: "I learned things about them I would have never learned no matter how long we would have ended up working together."

Three months later, the executive shared with his coach that their connections have only deepened—the way he interacts with these new employees and how they work with each other is qualitatively different from any other group he has ever worked with.

In a world of so much isolation and loneliness, getting back to the basics of Connecting can create profound shifts in how teams perform. Next, we will turn to the other overlooked yet foundational discipline of inclusive teams: Caring.

CHAPTER 1 SUMMARY

- Connecting is the ability to deeply understand and value the capabilities, professional experiences, and identity-forming biography of each team member.

- Showing professional curiosity builds deeper connections within a team, making team members feel seen and valued. A good way to achieve this is by incorporating The Three Questions.

- Team members within a diverse team may struggle with trust due to past experiences with discrimination and other forms of exclusion, whether professional or personal.

- Inclusive team members get to know and connect with every team member and not just those that are more like them.

- A shared purpose supports team collaboration and motivation to achieve.

CONNECTING TIPS

Host knowledge-sharing sessions. Organize regular sessions where team members can share expertise and insights from their respective business functions or about industry trends. These sessions can be added to existing meetings on the team's calendar or scheduled as their own stand-alone events. Creating such forums will help increase the breadth of exchanges on the team and create a fertile ground for innovation and problem solving.

Get back to analog. Disconnect from technology occasionally and opt for technology-free meetings to foster deeper connections and creativity. Gather in a distraction-free environment, such as a conference room or outdoor space, and ask everyone to leave their devices behind. Without the distraction of screens, team members can engage more fully in discussions, listen more actively to one another, and brainstorm ideas more creatively. Consider organizing the chairs in a circle without tables to promote inclusion and equality among members.

Trust walks. Organize trust walks where team members are paired up and blindfolded while navigating a predetermined path together. The sighted partner guides their blindfolded teammate, fostering communication, cooperation, and trust. After the walk, facilitate a debriefing session where participants discuss their experiences, emphasizing the importance of trust, vulnerability, and reliance on one another.

■　　■　　■

2

Discipline 2:
Caring to Nurture
Psychological Safety

No matter what happens in life, be good to people.
—Taylor Swift, pop artist

WHEN THE BOMBS STARTED FALLING ON KYIV, the entire Warsaw office stopped what they were doing to tend to the Ukrainian refugees arriving in Poland . . .

When the latest mass shooting was announced on the news, hundreds reached out to the colleague who had been in the middle of it with the dead surrounding them . . .

When a loved one was arrested in another country for being gay, dozens dug into their networks to find advocates in governments and human rights organizations that could get them home safely . . .

When someone fell on the floor in an epileptic attack, their teammates moved into action, knowing exactly how to support them . . .

CARING

The ability of team members to demonstrate personal concern for one another as well as for the team as an entity.

∎

When #AsianHate became a terrifying trend, coworkers reached out in concern to make sure their Asian colleagues got to and from work safely . . .

When Covid locked us in, we checked in with one another, shared health tips and condolences, and toasted over *quarantinis* on Zoom . . .

When George Floyd was murdered, so many the world over said *basta* and turned their rage and horror into allyship . . .

If there was ever a time for team members to show more care for each other, it's now. With 24/7 connectivity allowing us unfettered access to all the wrongs being committed in the world, mental health has been in a well-documented decline. *Forbes* found that in 2022, 23.1 percent of US adults (59.3 million) experienced a mental health condition and 19.1 million adults in the United States ages 19 to 54 experienced an anxiety disorder.[1] Overall, our workforce is in a less-than-optimal state of mind to perform or to even want to be present. And for those who must navigate through sexism, racism, ableism, homophobia, and other forms of discrimination and exclusion, the stresses are magnified. This is why the second discipline of inclusive teams, Caring, is of heightened importance.

While Connecting is *the ability to understand and value the professional experiences and identity-forming biography of each team member*, it alone cannot create the optimal conditions for effective collaboration and performance within teams.

Teams also need to care for one another.

CARING WITHIN INCLUSIVE TEAMS

We define Caring as *the ability to demonstrate personal concern for one another as well as for the team as an entity.*

Teams everywhere are becoming more diverse and employees' expectations of working in a place where they feel cared for are rising. It's no surprise, then, that a lack of belonging at work or connection with coworkers is a growing reason why employees quit their jobs. EY's 2023 Empathy in Business Survey showed that 50 percent of US workers surveyed left a previous job because they didn't feel like they belonged, and 42 percent because they had difficulty connecting with colleagues.[2] And according to a study published in *McKinsey Quarterly*, 86 percent of White women and 70 percent of women of color said they were likely to consider leaving their jobs if they did not feel a certain level of value or respect for their life circumstances.[3]

While it may be tempting to dismiss Caring as too basic a concept to spend too much time on in our hypercompetitive and demanding workplaces, it's not. Caring activates and energizes the connections between team members. It moves people past pleasantries and professional respect and toward the emotional and interpersonal engagement needed for teams to do their best work.

And while Caring may likewise seem like too basic a concept to devote an entire chapter to, too many leaders, managers, and teammates are not doing the fundamentals, to the detriment of team members' well-being as well as their collective work performance.

But let's be clear. The discipline of Caring is not about work teams becoming support groups in the psychological healing sense. Rather it is a call for teams to create the *psychological safety* people need to perform their best.

NURTURING PSYCHOLOGICAL SAFETY

Psychological safety was popularized in the 2000s by behavioral scientist and Harvard Business School professor Amy Edmondson, who defined it as "a shared belief among team members that the team is safe for interpersonal risk-taking." In teams that nurture psychological safety, their members feel safe to voice their opinions, ask judgment-free questions, and admit to mistakes without fear of punishment or humiliation.[4]

At Korn Ferry, we felt it important to underscore the role of psychological safety in diverse and inclusive teams; therefore, we see psychological safety as feeling free to be yourself and to contribute without fear of repercussion—*regardless of who you are.*

Clearly, environments that feel psychologically safe to some may not feel safe for others. And what it takes to feel psychologically safe in a team can vary significantly based on people's identities and how they may be perceived by others, especially when one person shares less in common with the majority in the group.

In a skeptical, cynical, prove-it-to-me world, achieving psychological safety is a tall order. But the rewards for teams who do so are exponential. Teams who experience higher psychological safety report higher learning behavior, increased employee engagement and motivation, and better decision-making.

Korn Ferry's research strongly supports these findings. Korn Ferry's 2024 engagement survey database, which comprises 225 global organizations and nearly 1 million employees, shows a clear correlation between a psychologically safe environment and employee engagement.[5] Employees who feel they can be themselves at work are substantially more engaged than those who don't feel free to be themselves (94 percent versus 51 percent). Similarly, those who report being able to freely express their views on work-related topics without fear of negative consequences are more engaged than those who are not (85 percent versus 34 percent). What's more, there is a notable relationship between psychological safety and employees' intent to stay (table 1).

Ultimately, a more collaborative and inclusive culture emerges in psycho-logically safe environments. This is because when managers create team environments where asking questions, proposing new ideas, and learning from mistakes is welcomed, team members feel freer to take interpersonal risks.[6] Connecting the dots between high performance and innovation, team members who feel safe to take risks are the ones most likely to rise to the full height of their abilities and to present new outlier ideas. It's quite the virtuous chain reaction that gets triggered by nurturing psychological safety!

Table 1 Psychological safety versus tenure

	EMPLOYEES INTENDING TO STAY WITH ORGANIZATION FOR MORE THAN 5 YEARS	EMPLOYEES THINKING OF LEAVING IN THE NEXT 12 MONTHS
I feel able to be myself at work.	88%	58%
I can freely express my views on work-related topics without fear of negative consequences.	73%	41%

(Korn Ferry, 2024)

Traditionally, psychological safety is measured at the team level, but the Korn Ferry Index goes a few steps further to measure it along three dimensions: Self, Team, and Organization.

- Self: Individuals' perceptions of feeling free to be themselves and speak up, without fear.
- Team: How well team members create an environment that nurtures psychological safety, providing support and enabling each other to be their authentic selves.
- Organization: To what extent the organization has modeled and created processes that support psychological safety.

Measuring this way enables leaders to pause and understand the many different levers that can be pulled to enable employees, teams, and their organizations to thrive. For example, one indicator of psychological safety at the *organizational* level is the degree to which employees perceive the process for handling complaints of mistreatment to be trustworthy. But if we look at this indicator by racial or ethnic group, what emerges can be seen in table 2. Tables 3 and 4 illustrate some examples of the disparities among different sex and gender orientations.

Furthermore, for nearly every one of our indicators, when we disaggregated the data by management level, the scores trended increasingly negative from top management to non-management, reinforcing the notion that leaders and employees in the same organization often have vastly different experiences of psychological safety.

Table 2 Psychological safety by race and ethnicity

Trust in company's process for handling mistreatment complaints						
ASIAN/ ASIAN AMERICAN	LATINX	WHITE	NATIVE HAWAIIAN AND PACIFIC ISLANDER (NHPI)	INDIGENOUS	TWO OR MORE RACES	BLACK
72%	71%	67%	64%	61%	60%	58%

(Korn Ferry, 2024)

Table 3 Psychological safety by gender and LGBTQ+ identity

Feel free to be myself at work				
MALE	FEMALE	STRAIGHT	LGBTQ+	NONBINARY*
84%	83%	85%	76%	54%

(Korn Ferry, 2024)

Table 4 Psychological safety by gender and LGBTQ+ identity

Trust in company's process for handling mistreatment complaints				
MALE	FEMALE	STRAIGHT	LGBTQ+	NONBINARY*
69%	62%	65%	56%	55%

(Korn Ferry, 2024)

Given psychological safety's deep implications for individual, team, and organizational performance, our findings underscore the need to understand what psychological safety means to people at all levels and from all groups represented within an organization.

Next we will explore the two key practices to the discipline of Caring: *Having Empathy* and *Being Mindful.* In figure 5 we illustrate that as various factors weigh down team members based on their identities, Caring is the antidote to the debilitating effects these can have. Caring comprises two practices, empathy and mindfulness, as ways to effectively demonstrate Caring. When activated and practiced these can turn the negative inputs into constructive outcomes.

HAVING EMPATHY

There are many benefits stemming from an empathetic workplace, including greater efficiency, creativity, job satisfaction, idea sharing, innovation, productivity, and even company revenue. Further, it inspires positive change within the workplace, mutual respect between employees and leaders, and reduced employee turnover.[7]

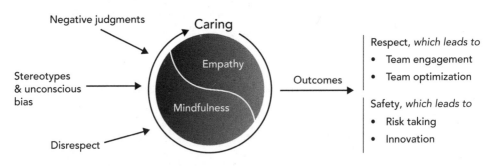

Figure 5: Empathy and Mindfulness Model (Korn Ferry, 2024)

In a major disconnect, however, while 92 percent of CEOs feel their organization is empathetic, only 50 percent of their employees say their CEO is empathetic.[8]

There are, of course, CEOs who get it, and live it. The CEO of a company Michel consults with kicks off a day on leadership development for a group of thirty leaders. From the front of the room, he explains why he's investing in their development. "I care about you and your growth. I hope this program will equip you for all that life may throw your way, not just in the halls of this company." Saying it aloud to the group has a visceral impact. His communication is genuine and clear. He backs up the words with tangible actions. No wonder his people rank their culture and his leadership highly in survey after survey.

Contrast this with a leader Andrés coached who grew up with a father and two brothers with multiple sclerosis (MS). Their life expectancies were in the single digits and yet they lived more than twenty years past their predicted life spans. Yet, given her organization's culture of drawing boundaries around personal disclosures, no one in her workplace of over twenty-five years knew about her family situation, despite it being one of the single greatest influences in how she lived her life and led at work.

Drawing from the field of psychology, there are three types of empathy, all of which are applicable to the discipline of Caring: affective empathy, compassionate empathy, and cognitive empathy.

AFFECTIVE EMPATHY

Affective empathy is demonstrated by words and body language that express care and concern as a crucial aspect of human social interaction.[9] The practices around affective empathy are among the best known but not necessarily the most used. Which of these do you recognize, and which do you practice?

Spoken Language:

- "It's completely understandable that you feel that way given what you've been through."
- "I'm truly sorry you're experiencing this; it must be incredibly hard."
- "That sounds incredibly frustrating; I would feel the same in your shoes."

- "I'm here for you, whatever you need."
- "I'm incredibly moved/saddened/affected by your situation."

Body Language:

- Reflecting the emotional state of the person through your facial expressions and body language, such as nodding and showing concern or sadness in your face when they share distressing news.
- Offering any culturally and situationally appropriate physical touch to convey support and understanding.
- Remaining present in the situation by sitting silently with the person in their time of need, giving them your full attention.
- Actively listening without interrupting, making judgmental comments, or rushing to give advice.

By empathizing with the life circumstances of individuals in this way, leaders can foster a supportive environment where team members feel comfortable expressing their thoughts and emotions without fear of judgment. This type of Caring helps build stronger relationships within the team, leading to better collaboration, enhanced communication, and increased overall effectiveness.[10]

COMPASSIONATE EMPATHY

Compassionate empathy goes beyond understanding and sharing emotions to include a genuine desire to act and to alleviate the suffering of others or simply to help them in some way. Not surprisingly, affective empathy is often the gateway to compassionate empathy.

Active listening is vital in compassionate empathy. Why? Because it's not compassionate to jump in and help before we take the time to clearly understand what the challenges and the person's needs are—not just what

---

PARADOX: CARING CAN LEAD TO A LOWER FOCUS ON RESULTS!

Learn more in chapter 6.

■

---

we think they need. To do so we must attune ourselves to their verbal and nonverbal messages.

Ironically, while the person operating in affective and compassionate empathy is not seeking a benefit, they usually gain one anyway. Neuroscience has shown that when anyone offers a listening ear and does something for others, it releases a cocktail of hormones, including oxytocin, dopamine, and serotonin—all of which contribute positively to the giver's mood, captured in the concept of a "helpers' high." *(For more, see Neuroscience Corner.)*

NEUROSCIENCE CORNER

Caring's Multiplier Effect

Amelia Haynes

When we experience a social threat, such as one to our security, status, fairness, autonomy, or trust, our brains go into a state of heightened alert, increasing production of cortisol, adrenaline, or epinephrine, thereby escalating stress, mistrust, hostility, and disgust. In fact, studies show that the brain processes social pain as though it were physical pain. And our empathy with someone else's pain can activate the same part of our brains (the insula) as when we personally experience pain, in a process known as secondary trauma.

Yet the opposite is also true. We can decrease threat responses by appealing to positive domains of social experience, including caring for and feeling cared for by others. When we perceive caring, our brains produce more oxytocin and serotonin, which in turn boosts collaboration, cohesiveness, trust, and empathy. While perceived threats trigger the brain's primary threat circuitry, caring relation-ships trigger neurotransmitters involved in the reward circuitry.

Oxytocin helps us form social attachments and trust. *Dopamine*, involved in reward, motivation, and pleasure, enhances prosocial behaviors, such as generosity, altruism, and moral behavior, by making us feel good when we help others. *Serotonin* increases our positive mood and reduces our negative emotions. *Glutamate* helps us with perspective-taking and understanding the mental states of others.

With all the benefits of activating this hormonal cocktail, it is no surprise that employees practicing Caring with their team members works.

CARING FOR A TEAM MEMBER WITH A HIDDEN DISABILITY

When My Epilepsy Throws Me on the Floor

Matt Norquist

The first time I woke up on the ground in my office, with a crowd of people looking at me and paramedics checking my pulse and blood pressure, was mortifying.

Over the next few years, it has happened nearly twenty more times. And it can still happen at any moment. My affliction? Epilepsy. It manifests through something called "tonic-clonic" seizures that make you fall, shake, froth at the mouth, and bite your tongue, among other symptoms.

I, as well as those close to me at home and at work, have learned a lot about what to do and how to deal with the aftermath. I have also had a chance to sort through my many conflicted feelings and thoughts on the topic.

At first, I was very focused on making my disability less of an imposition on others. I wanted to make sure no one felt uncomfortable or awkward. That was nice of me—too nice! While it's important for my family and coworkers to be educated on my condition, I realized after a while that whether they felt uncomfortable was their responsibility, not mine.

As a mission- and business-driven leader who likes to win financially as well as bring about positive change, I thought my impairment would ruin my credibility, harm my ability to be seen as powerful, and hinder my potential to advance. In some ways it has—but in other ways it hasn't.

In fact, my disability has become a special ability.

The Downsides

I do have a more limited bandwidth. I can't work as much, I need more sleep and to watch my stress, and I have be cautious about pushing it. For my type A personality, this is a good thing for my overall health, but it hasn't been easy to accept or manage. I have had to learn how.

The medications make me slower. They mess up my memory and hamper a number of the things that were my greatest strengths.

I need to inform people about my disability. It's embarrassing every time I have to do it, especially when most people don't really know what to say.

If I don't share, and people around me don't know, when it happens, it's pandemonium. Most people don't have experience with helping someone having a seizure and the sight of someone going through it, I understand, can be scary. Most people, rather than stepping away, do seek to do something but often they don't know what that should be. Many revert to helplessly feeling sorry for me, asking me incessantly how I'm doing even days after the episode. It's sweet, but it makes me feel like a loser.

The Upsides

I remain an ALL-OUT person. Like the decathlete I used to be, which required me to do ten events over two days, I have learned to do what I need to do in spurts rather than trying to go nonstop. Instead, I do the sprint-walk-sprint-walk mode of work. Stress is my biggest trigger for seizures, so I choose not to get stressed.

It has also really helped me be a much more empathetic leader. I've become really tuned in to other invisible disabilities such as autism, being hard of hearing, blindness, early-stage Parkinson's, addiction, mental health issues, gambling, and so forth.

By the way, about 5 percent of the US workforce has a disability, which translates into 9 million people. And this number is underreported because many choose to not disclose their disability given concerns about job security. But, of course, it's not just people with disability who face adversity. Everywhere there are people who struggle to get through their days for all kinds of reasons that we can't see.

My invisible disability has motivated me to be more curious about who people are and tuned in to when they may need help for something that is not directly work related. But everything *is* work related anyway. If a team member is stressed or hurting for any reason, it will affect their work. And in the same way that I need understanding and accommodation, so do they, so I try to do something about it. This requires me being available temporally and emotionally for team members to confide in me.

(continued)

CARING FOR A TEAM MEMBER WITH A HIDDEN DISABILITY

(continued)

Also, my being part of an inclusive team has made all the difference. My team members are my superheroes. They were the ones who quickly got me out of harm's way the first time—calling 911, then my wife, and cleaning up the mess.

As a leader who explicitly needs help from those around me, I am better able to see the skills and potential of people on my team as well as be witness to their caring spirits. Kelly Gruber on my team takes the most accurate notes. Stewart Clarke makes sure nobody bothers me in the aftermath of an episode so I can get my work done. Christina, Sam, Jon, and Angela have become experts on what to do: calling an ambulance and reaching out to my wife, getting me a sugary drink when I come back around, and giving me a ride back home if I feel wobbly. I am so grateful to them.

Before I knew I had a disability I walked past so many people. Now I see them in new and real ways.

COGNITIVE EMPATHY

Cognitive empathy is less about emotional caring and more about an intellectual appreciation of someone else's circumstances—our ability to put ourselves in someone else's shoes and to see the world from their vantage point. This is often referred to as *perspective taking*. By actively engaging in perspective taking, we can transcend our own biases and assumptions, gaining a deeper understanding of others' thoughts, feelings, and motivations.

Cognitive empathy allows for more effective collaboration and complex decision-making across functions. Consider the following story about a global, high-prestige medical devices company where it took a diverse team using cognitive empathy to finally crack the code on a quality issue that had plagued them for nearly twenty years.[11]

A critical monitoring instrument in the intensive care unit was not lasting as long as it was supposed to in 15 percent of instances, prompting dissatisfaction in the market. For the world's leading supplier of this instrument, this was a significant problem. After nearly twenty years of consistent yet unsuccessful troubleshooting, the company formed a special-project team that drew from more diverse parts of the organization. By design, the leader was not an engineer or scientist, but someone from the accounting department with a predisposition to probe from unexpected points of view.

The first action the leader took was to bring in an interdisciplinary team that included talent from marketing, HR, and supply chain, among other functions. The core technical experts were complemented by newly graduated engineers who learned under different and more contemporary paradigms. The upgraded team also had a more global profile to break the overrepresentation of members from the country in which headquarters was located.

The team had to deliberately develop cognitive empathy toward one another because their backgrounds and expertise were quite varied. Without an understanding of others' perspectives, skill sets, and experiences, the potential for paralysis and infighting due to their vast diversity was exceptionally high.

By leaning on each other with a default cognitive appreciation for their differences, the team fostered a sense of psychological safety, enabling individual members to express their ideas and concerns without fear of judgment. Engineers valued the non-engineers in the group for the complementary credentials and experiences they had rather than dismissing them for not being technical. Together, they built a shared understanding of the problem, the potential solutions, and their implications across functions. They began to identify synergies, trade-offs, and creative compromises that balanced the diverse needs of each function.

Then came breakthrough.

One team member challenged their working premise. For twenty years they had tried to solve the problem by focusing on why the device was failing prematurely 15 percent of the time.

"What if instead we focus on figuring out why it's working *correctly* 85 percent of the time?"

This reframing of the problem made all the difference. It led to the discovery of the deep engineering root cause that then led to the fix. Having extended cognitive empathy toward one another—embracing and creating space for each other's diverse experiences, backgrounds, and perspectives—made all the difference.

BEING MINDFUL

One of the last things hard-charging teams ever think about is taking the time to slow down. Work is simply too demanding in a go-go-go world. In fact, it's often the team environment itself, in all its hyperactivity, competitive drive, and ambition, that fuels the constant forward press toward the next deliverable or event.

This type of hard-charging environment is not conducive to nurturing a psychologically safe environment.

Caring simply can't be done on the fly. To take in what someone is sharing from the heart, to support them through their trauma, and to put ourselves in their shoes requires *us to be in the moment* with them. While many practitioners of mindfulness focus on doing it for themselves for their own sake (a very healthy thing to do!), here we focus on the practice of mindfulness within teams for the sake of all team members.

To live out the practice of mindfulness in the pursuit of Caring, we must pause, center, and reset.

PAUSE

Our Korn Ferry colleague Kevin Cashman wrote the best-selling book *The Pause Principle*, which explores how leaders leverage "the pause" to lead themselves, their teams, and their organizations.[12] Cashman defined the pause as a conscious, intentional process of stepping back to reflect and deliberate, allowing one to then move forward with greater clarity and impact. He posited that the pause is an antidote to our addiction to speed and transaction, and that it's only when we pause that we can do things differently.

Cashman explains:

> For most, slowing down to drive performance is counter to instinct, especially when they have been rewarded for speed and action. But stepping forward to act, particularly in complex situations, without first stepping back for information, clarity, and connection to what is most important can be disastrous.

In his book, Cashman presented pausing practices for individuals such as meditation, micro retreats, longer sabbaticals, and even fifteen-second pauses before speaking or acting—that's the length of time it takes to move from an amygdala flight-or-fight response to a conscious, thoughtful, deliberate one coming from the prefrontal cortex. Here, we offer how inclusive teams make mindful pauses a practice.

Inclusive teams harness their obsession for planning and execution to ensure that pauses are thoughtfully designed and scheduled ahead of time. They mix up the types of pauses: built-in pauses before weekly meetings to check in with each other personally; monthly pauses to have conversations reflecting not the work itself, but on how they are interacting with each other in doing the work; and quarterly or semiannual pauses to constructively evaluate team progress toward their common purpose. When the inevitable conflict arises, rather than allowing the tension to send the team into an emotional vortex, they call a timeout to lean away from the conflict, take a breath, and regain perspective. And then they center and reset, which we discuss next.

CENTER

There can be such a thing as too much teaming. Constantly being amid the neurotransmitter electrical currents of others can fray and fry us. We all need some time to ourselves to rest, relieve stress, connect with our inner selves, and reflect on all the interaction and feedback inherent to a group setting. When we center, we take a much-needed individual timeout to recharge our focus and energy. We care for ourselves so we are better able to care for others.

John is a hard-driving executive and a committed family man. He works hard and plays hard. One morning on a route he takes every day, a car in his blind spot careened into him, sending his car into two 360-degree spins. John was not physically hurt, and after exchanging insurance information with the other driver he made his way to work. But as he sat in his office to begin his day, he realized he simply could not focus.

John called his wife to tell her what happened.

"So, what are you doing being at the office right now?" she asked.

"Uh, working," he answered.

"No, you need to be home right now and let your psyche reset. You experienced trauma and even a strong man like you is not immune."

Not out of conviction, but out of trust of his partner's love and care as well as her area of expertise as a mindfulness coach, he went home. When he got home, the emotions came out, through tears and some sharing.

He needed a moment or two. He needed to pause, to center. He needed to be mindful.

We simply don't do enough of this. As we rush through the days—stressful as they usually are—cortisol levels keep rising and yet we keep plowing through. Eventually the unmanaged stress can no longer be suppressed. We make basic errors, we snap, and in the process we undermine both our and our team's sense of well-being and psychological safety.

NEUROSCIENCE CORNER

Centering Really Works

Amelia Haynes

Not only does centering help us with managing stress, but it also helps us manage the automaticity of unconscious biases, one of the most substantial underminers of Caring in an inclusive team. Research shows centering in the form of meditation improves self-regulation in terms of response inhibition[13] and reduces automatic evaluation and forms of automatic social cognition.[14]

Contact theory proposes that frequent interaction with people from different races will change the formation of the in-group, which will reduce bias. But differences are exceptionally challenging. They are difficult to process and internalize and accept in the moment. Centering alone is a powerful and necessary step to absorb new learnings, to become more self-aware of our own resistances, and to recognize the need for more information.

Neuroscience explains that automaticity is often a function of environmental cues, so changing our context—especially by withdrawing for a moment—can effectively change our behavior.

It is no wonder then that self-awareness, aided by centering, was particularly helpful for around 50 percent of research respondents when working with others in a team, acting as a coach, dealing with change, and managing and leading others.[15]

Until we are pulled together, until we practice self-care, we can't be part of pulling a team together. By not allowing ourselves and our teammates the time to center, we undermine team inclusiveness.

RESET

To reset is to change direction—slightly or radically—to get unstuck from corroding conflict, from plans that are not yielding the desired results, or from dead-end attempts at innovation.

Team resetting requires collective *self-awareness* to recognize the behaviors that may be perpetuating a lack of results. Research has found that although 95 percent of people think they're self-aware, only 10 to 15 percent are! In a survey conducted of 467 working adults in the United States across several industries, 99 percent reported working with at least one such person, and nearly half worked with at least four. Peers were the most frequent offenders (with 73 percent of respondents reporting at least one unaware peer), followed by direct reports (33 percent), bosses (32 percent), and clients (16 percent).[16]

Un-self-aware colleagues aren't just frustrating; they can cut a team's chances of success in half, reports organizational psychologist Dr. Tasha Eurich.[17] In her book *Insight: Why We're Not as Self-Aware as We Think, and How Seeing Ourselves Clearly Helps Us Succeed at Work and in Life,* she delves into the connection between a lack of self-awareness and team dysfunction.[18] She writes that un-self-aware individuals won't listen to or accept critical feedback, can't empathize with or take the perspective of others, have difficulty "reading a room" and tailoring their message to their audience, possess an inflated opinion of their contributions and performance, are hurtful to others without realizing it, and take credit for successes and blame others for failures.

Here again we press beyond the foundational research based on the *individual* to extend its application to *teams*. While being self-aware as an individual is a first step, team members must be team-aware. Team self-awareness can provide perspective outside our peripheral vision on the part of trusted people. The practices related to the disciplines of Connecting and Caring lend themselves to greater team self-awareness. For example, when we have built trust and created psychological safety, we are better positioned to offer and receive

SCRIPTS FOR RESETTING

- Acknowledge the need for a reset, openly recognizing any tension or challenges within the team.

- Initiate individual reflection, allowing team members to consider recent experiences, interactions, and personal contributions.

- Open an honest dialogue where team members can express concerns, share feedback, and discuss any issues impacting team dynamics.

- Realign the team's goals and objectives to ensure clarity and collective understanding. Confirm that everyone is on the same page regarding priorities and expectations.

- Commit as a team to sustain a positive team culture, encouraging a solutions-oriented mindset and a supportive atmosphere to enhance collaboration and productivity.

---

constructive feedback from others. We believe that we are all in this together and that the reset is intended for the collective success and well-being of the team.

A team's ability to collectively introspect is key to working through sticking points, to backing out of dead ends, and to repairing frayed nerves during times of tension. And it is only once the team has reset that they can work together to leave the rest stop and get back on the road to results at full speed.

PULLING IT ALL TOGETHER

In the wake of Argentina's devastating tournament-opening loss to Saudi Arabia during the 2022 Qatar World Cup, their coach, Lionel Scaloni, rejected the old-school coaching style of shaming players into higher performance. Instead, he paved the way with his Caring response. As the shock of the upset reverberated around the world and press and fans went after the Argentine team, Scaloni's response was neither dismay nor disapproval. Instead, he stood firm in his belief in his team, shielding his players from the storm of criticism.

"This is a strong group," Scaloni said. "Today wasn't our day, but I am confident in our team and our journey ahead."

Team captain Lionel Messi also stepped up to echo the Caring ethos that Scaloni had nurtured within the squad: "We lift each other up. That's what teams do."

The moment of loss became a catalyst, not for blame or division, but for an even stronger consolidation of team spirit. First-time starter Julián Álvarez, whose inclusion in the lineup had drawn criticism from the media and fans, added, "In this team, everyone has your back. That's the kind of support that drives you to give your best."

And midfielder Rodrigo De Paul said, "There's something special about this group. We share every moment, every challenge, every triumph together."

Rather than fracturing the squad, the setback against Saudi Arabia served as a reminder of their unwavering support for one another.

The Argentine team went on a tear after that. They won every game that followed. They celebrated on the pitch after each win as a tight, unified team—long after most teams would have retired to their locker rooms—and then with their fans, singing joyous chants. At the end, they lifted the Jules Rimet Trophy in Lusail Stadium after one of the most thrilling World Cup finals ever.

Argentina's success was not just a victory for the team but for the discipline of Caring they practiced so well. The team cultivated an environment in which every player felt valued, understood, and safe to take risks and make mistakes. They achieved their collective mission of winning a third World Cup for their country and helping Messi, arguably the world's best player, finally win soccer's most prestigious trophy.

Take this Caring spirit from the soccer pitch to the corporate world. When it comes to *Fortune*'s "100 Best Companies to Work For" and Glassdoor's list of the "2020 Best Places to Work," empathy reveals itself to be the mutual success sauce in the creation of winning enterprises with engaging cultures.

Now, with the disciplines of Connecting and Caring fully laid out, let's leverage those foundations to activate the other disciplines, starting with Synchronizing.

CHAPTER 2 SUMMARY

- Caring is the ability of team members to demonstrate personal concern for one another as well as for the team as an entity.

- Psychological safety is feeling free to be yourself and contribute without fear of repercussions, regardless of who you are.

- Mindfulness helps us be present in the moment, allowing teams to pause, center, and reset to address problems.

- Psychological safe spaces help increase mental well-being, a sense of belonging, and greater engagement and innovation.

- Empathy enables teams to better understand and relate to the experiences and emotions and perspectives of others for more effective collaboration and complex decision-making.

CARING TIPS

Adopt kindness as a team norm. Acknowledge and celebrate acts of kindness and compassion within the team. Start by having team members define what kindness means to them and what they would recommend doing to recognize it. Many teams use "shout-outs" in meetings to express gratitude, but for members uncomfortable with being singled out, more discreet practices may convey a greater sense of caring.

Build Caring into onboarding experiences. How teams address the various needs of their new members sends a clear signal about how much they prioritize Caring on the team. Ensure new members "feel the love" with a comprehensive onboarding plan that covers essential information, training modules, and introductions to all team members. Pair a new team member with a mentor or buddy who can provide guidance, support, and insider tips.

Extend Caring outside the physical workplace. Demonstrating Caring presents challenges as employees navigate remote work and in-office dynamics. Foster regular check-ins to maintain connection and support for both remote and in-person team members. Explore resources for improving work-from-home setups, such as ergonomic assessments and stipends for equipment. Implement time management tools and techniques to help employees balance their workloads effectively, including setting clear boundaries between work and personal time.

3

Discipline 3: *Synchronizing* to Harness Collective Intelligence

I've never scored a goal in my life
without getting a pass from someone else.
—Abby Wambach, member of the
USA Women's National Soccer Team
and 2015 FIFA Women's
World Cup champion

HUNDREDS OF THOUSANDS OF STARLINGS FLY in unison doing hairpin turns at eighty kilometers per hour. As they ebb and flow, shape-shift, change direction, zoom up, dive down, and slide sideways in perfect synchronicity, their flapping wings generate a vibration called murmuration. This collective intelligence mechanism allows myriad

SYNCHRONIZING

The state of being coordinated in time and purpose, where multiple elements or entities align collaboratively and harmoniously through systems, networks, and devices.

teams of seven birds in tight, equidistant formations to operate as the neural and physical coordination nodes for the entire flock.[1]

We humans have this capacity for synchronicity too.

It can be witnessed while sitting in the middle of the Argentine fandom at a World Cup match or standing at the front of the stage of a sold-out Beyonce concert—pulsating waves of people singing the same songs with the same inflections while thrusting their fists into the air in unison, chests held up, voices dialed to max volume. That's the power, beauty, and exhalation of human synchronicity.

In ancient Rome, phalanxes—collections of small, well-integrated, well-coordinated groups arrayed in checkerboard formation (not unlike the starling formation structure)—allowed for optimal militaristic synchronicity. And religious and community organizations have long engaged in Synchronizing activities, such as marching, singing, and dancing, that lead group members to engage in more complex coordinate actions.

In less exuberant ways, we can have the same type of experience with an inspirational speaker in a corporate crowd at an ERG summit. Or as part of a team brainstorming in front of a whiteboard as the "ahas" burst forth. Or as part of a software development agile scrum or a problem-solving hackathon.

Synchronous activity generates coordinated physical, electrical, and hormonal reactions and produces positive emotions that weaken the psychological barriers between the self, the group, and the groups within groups. This is what makes Synchronizing such a powerful discipline of inclusive teams. It is the ability to synchronize that unlocks a team's collective intelligence, transforming a regular group of individuals into a high-impact inclusive team.

■   ■   ■

In their breakthrough book on collective intelligence, *The Knowledge Illusion: Why We Never Think Alone,* authors Steven Sloman and Philip Fernbach explain the power of synchronicity:

> People are like bees and society a beehive: Our intelligence resides not in individual brains but in the collective mind. To function, individuals rely not only on knowledge stored within our skulls but also on knowledge stored elsewhere: in our bodies, in the environment, and especially in other people. When you put it all together, human thought is incredibly impressive. But it is a product of a community, not of any individual alone.[2]

Take the team that worked on the Event Horizon Telescope (EHT) project, obtaining the first image of a supermassive black hole.[3] That black hole, the same mass of 6.5 billion suns, is 50 million light years away in the Messier 87 galaxy, sucking up whole planets and stars as they cross its event horizon. The team's seemingly impossible goal: to capture an image of a phenomenon from which not even light can escape.

The EHT team of about two hundred scientists from around the world achieved this goal by synchronizing observations from six radio telescopes anchored in the South Pole, the Atacama Desert in Chile, mountains in the Arizona desert, volcanoes in Mexico and Hawaii, and in the Sierra Nevada of Spain. Shep Doeleman, the global director of the EHT project, explained how this "very-long-baseline interferometry" technique works: "We take telescopes scattered around the world and make them all look simultaneously at the black hole. Imagine taking a mirror, smashing it with a hammer and distributing these shards worldwide. And then recording what happens on each of those shards and then bringing them together and reconstructing that mirror in a supercomputer."[4]

Once the telescopes were aligned and coordinated, teams of scientists had to mirror the telescopes' synchronicity with human synchronicity as they captured the data nearly simultaneously—for five consecutive sleepless days and nights. Every facet of the project, from data processing to algorithm development, bore the imprint of synchronized teamwork.

The team succeeded in creating the equivalent of an earth-sized telescope with an aperture gigantic enough to capture the very faint and short-length radio waves being emitted by the black hole. But there was

NEUROSCIENCE CORNER

The Heart of Synchrony

Amelia Haynes

The brain operates using electrical signals. On a small scale, neurons communicate with one another using these electrical signals, either helped or hindered by neurotransmitters. But these processes operate on a large scale as well, supporting systems and processes that not only take place throughout the whole human body, but as scientists have recently learned, among the brains and bodies of multiple people. Hyper-scanning, the process of scanning the brain activity of more than one person at a time, has clued researchers into the fascinating interplay of the electrical patterns that help support communication both within different regions of the brain and with the brains of others.

This interplay is known as *interpersonal synchrony*. Synchrony arises from a combination of motor, sensory, and social cognitive neurological processes. It is both neurological and physiological. Much of the literature on interpersonal synchrony focuses on the phenomenon of behavior mirroring between two or more people.

However, some studies indicate that synchrony is more nuanced than this simple behavioral mimicry. It's not just that we copy someone else's body language, but under the surface, our neurological activity can become synced with the neurological, emotional, and physiological activity of someone with whom we are engaged in a cooperative activity.

For example, one study shows that observing the actions of others elicits neural synchrony in the motor cortex, and drumming with another person can cause the two heartbeats to match up. Sharing positive events or having vulnerable conversations can elicit synchrony in emotional expressions and experiences.

This research makes clear that synchrony is not limited to physical behaviors or movements but includes sensory, physical, physiological, linguistic, affective, and neural manifestations, which can ultimately lead to improved communication, greater degrees of affiliation, improved cooperation, and better decision-making.

still more work to do. After the capture, it took nearly two years of meticulous coordination by this diverse team to synthesize all the data to create the actual image of the black hole: a bright ring encircling a very dark central region. This monumental cosmic discovery was the result of an inclusive team of scientists worldwide putting aside local individual interests and idiosyncratic ways of working across language and time zone differences to deliver something astonishing.

SYNCHRONIZING WITHIN INCLUSIVE TEAMS

Interestingly, synchronizing *across differences* was not always valued. One of the first management consultants in the early era of industrialization, Frederick Taylor, promoted management principles designed for *rote* synchronicity. To maximize efficiency and productivity he suggested that processes be completed by the masses in the same exact way time after time, minimizing variability (referred to as *Taylorism*).

While this standardization did lead to increased output and reduced production budgets, thus enabling mass production on a scale previously unimaginable, it came at a high cost. Workers faced monotonous, repetitive tasks, leading to debilitating morale. The rigid adherence to a set process limited individual creativity and autonomy, stifling innovation and problem solving. This one-size-fits-all approach failed to consider the unique skills and capabilities of individual workers, sidelining talent assets (ironically) in the name of greater optimization. Socially, it reinforced a hierarchical work environment, with workers having little input or control over their work.

It was not until the late twentieth century that process innovators began to tap into the power of *differentiated* Synchronizing. Workplace application pioneers from a wide array of disciplines—psychology, organizational psychology, systems science, economics, IT, AI, and so on—drew from a wide array of fields far from the corporate space, such as quantum mechanics, philosophy, anthropology, sociology, theology, spirituality, biology, environmental science, the arts, literature, and sports, in their quest to optimize for individual differences. (They didn't call it "diversity," but the similarities are clear.)

They explored and continue to explore the optimal activation of human relationships and group dynamics that will create an experience greater than the sum of its parts. Twenty-first-century researchers Anita

Woolley, Ishani Aggarwal, and Thomas Malone refer to this phenomenon as *collective intelligence*, which they define as "a group's capacity to perform a wide array of tasks." Their definition implies that intelligence emerges from the collaboration and collective efforts of the group rather than from the individual abilities of its members. Neuroscientist Hannah Critchlow calls it *joined-up thinking*, explaining that "if we can nurture the combined brain power of the many, across groups and across generations by opening up to ancient wisdom, to intellectual mavericks and outlier ideas, we can shift from 'me' thinking to 'we' thinking."[5]

We can think of collective intelligence or joined-up thinking as the *what* and Synchronizing as the *how*. *Synchronizing* is being coordinated in time and purpose, with multiple elements or entities aligned collaboratively and harmoniously through standards, systems, and practices. This concept can be found across many different domains—a musical group, dual-process chips in laptops, a beehive—as they exemplify timed rhythmic coordination, multiple things happening at once, and friction-less interaction.

In inclusive work teams, Synchronizing manifests in collaborative decision-making and collaborative task execution, where members exhibit coordinated behaviors and shared emotional states via verbal and nonverbal communication. This synchrony integrates tasks, communication, and goals, fostering enhanced collaboration, increased speed, and greater efficiency.

In a synchronized team, members draw on each other's diverse strengths and experiences—their collective intelligence—to achieve shared objectives through shared purpose and mutual empathy.

Next, we will explore the critical practices that lead to Synchronizing.

- Finding the Team's Rhythm
- Having a Win-Together Mindset
- Storytelling

FINDING THE TEAM'S RHYTHM

The peloton in the Tour de France is the epitome of synchronicity. It moves up and down hills, valleys, and mountains, along smooth asphalt or rough cobblestone, in a continuously adjusting block of riders trading places, each mindful of everyone else's position and movements, to

HIDDEN FIGURES IN THE NICK OF TIME: SYNCHRONIZING REENTRY BACK TO EARTH

On February 20, 1962, as John Glenn orbited the earth aboard *Friendship 7*, a mathematical race against time unfolded at NASA's Langley Research Center, where the flight was being managed.

Tasked with calculating the spacecraft's precise reentry point into Earth's atmosphere, the mission's success hinged on the seamless execution and collaboration of the skilled engineering team at Langley, which included mathematicians Katherine Johnson, Dorothy Vaughan, and Mary Jackson, three African American women whose stories are told in the book and movie *Hidden Figures*.

Amid the high-stakes mission, discrepancies in the IBM computer's trajectory calculations emerged, threatening to jeopardize the mission. Glenn's spaceship had to be kept in proper alignment to enter the atmosphere at the necessary angle. Too steep and the spacecraft would burn up on reentry. Too shallow and it would skip off the atmosphere and back into space. Being off by just a few degrees either way could lead to tragedy.

Katherine Johnson, recognized for her meticulous accuracy, was called on to manually verify the calculations. Her swift recalculations, performed under immense pressure, provided the essential data needed for a safe reentry.

Meanwhile, Dorothy Vaughan was tasked with maintaining the reliability of the IBM systems. Her expertise in Fortran programming allowed her to make real-time adjustments, ensuring that the computational support was accurate and timely—an essential component amid the high stakes of the mission.

Elsewhere, Mary Jackson worked closely with the capsule's engineering team. Her expertise in aerodynamics was critical to ensuring the heat shields designed to protect Glenn against the intense heat of reentry did their job. Her recommendations on the shields' design and integrity were swiftly implemented, ensuring the structural safety of the spacecraft during its descent.

John Glenn, only the third human to ever orbit the earth, was fully aware of the critical support being provided by the ground team. He expressed his deep trust and confidence in their capabilities.

The coordinated efforts of the team paid off and the capsule successfully reentered Earth's atmosphere, splashing down safely off Grand Turk Island, north of the Dominican Republic.

Synchronicity had saved the day.

optimize performance. They employ both *structure* and *spontaneity* to enter into synchronicity.

STRUCTURE

The necessary structures to establish a team's rhythm are clear roles and responsibilities, effective and open communication channels, and a well-defined scope of work.

Clear roles and responsibilities create an organized and synchronized workflow, minimizing the chances of misalignment and ensuring each team member's efforts fit seamlessly within the broader objectives. Clear roles that include meaningful contributions foster a profound sense of accountability among team members. When individuals understand the direct impact of their contributions on the team's success, they are more likely to take ownership of their responsibilities.

Effective and open communication channels promote unity, mutual respect, and a collective commitment to the organization's mission. They ensure everyone is on the same page and reduce misunderstandings. Team members who are kept informed of the context in which they do their work *and* feel their opinions are heard and valued are much more likely to work cohesively toward shared objectives.

A well-defined scope of work leaves no room for ambiguity and minimizes the likelihood of tasks falling through the cracks. This clarity not only enhances individual accountability but also sets the stage for more efficient collaboration, contributing significantly to the overall efficiency and success of the team.

SPONTANEITY

But structure alone can suffocate through rigidity. Remember the example of rote synchronicity promoted by Frederick Taylor?

Within an inclusive team, there needs to be a clear distinction between *high standardization* (getting work done via structure) and *high coordination* (getting work done in coordinated spontaneity).

If you're not a jazz expert, you may think of the musical style as free-flowing and lacking rules. But what allows a jazz band to create beautiful and synchronized improvisational pieces is a mastery of both structure and spontaneity. In jazz, synchronicity depends on mastering various structural concepts. For example, the well-known "I-ii-V-I" jazz

> # PARADOX: SYNCHRONIZING REQUIRES A DEGREE OF ASYNCHRONY!
>
> *Learn more in chapter 6.*

chord progression creates a sense of musical resolution by taking the listener on a journey from home (the I chord) to two different places (the ii chord and the V chord) before returning home (I chord again). Such structure is the musical equivalent of the roles and responsibilities, channels of communication, and scope of work in inclusive teams.

With the solid foundation of this structure, the jazz band can now begin to riff. Both jazz bands and inclusive teams can find their spontaneous flow by continuous pinging, having an adaptable mindset, and personalization.

Continuous Pinging

Continuous pinging is how inclusive team members stay in rhythm with each other. Weekly and even daily updates, as well as long emails, have their place in the structural rhythms. But to maintain spontaneous rhythm inclusive teams need Slack, Teams, WhatsApp, texts, and, yes, calls. These tools facilitate the call and response of team members working to remain in alignment.

While so many modes of instantaneous communication can be overwhelming, intrusive, and interrupting, the work of the inclusive team is to master this continuous pinging as they improvise throughout the day to get the work done. With a word, a phrase, or a thumbs-up, hear, or heart emoji, they send just the right amount of info to keep the team in sync *and* calibrated to change key without missing a beat, or to leverage a new opportunity without losing sight of the main objective. Check, check, check. All systems go. Stop. Pause. Switch. Go. Okay. This is the spontaneous rhythm of musicians, astronauts, and nurses and doctors—inclusive teams of all kinds.

By the way, we'd like to mention one thing about calls we've learned in our work: Inclusive teams would do well to pick up the phone sometimes.

The rapid fire of texts, WhatsApp messages, and emojis keep it all flowing fast. But sometimes, digitally deconstructed communications can trap us in a loop of misunderstanding. An actual group phone or video call can go a long way to getting a team back in the groove.

An Adaptable Mindset

An adaptable mindset ensures that leaders and their teams can respond quickly and effectively when internal or external forces, or pings from the team, signal a change in demand. Some examples include new disruptive competitors, high inflation, supply chain disruption, a team member leaving, an organizational restructure through a merger and acquisition (M&A), or a move to self-serve employee benefits.

Adaptability requires a willingness to pivot strategies and tactics and swiftly embrace new ideas. Consider Yum! Brands' all-out pivot from customers taking orders at the counter to ordering from a kiosk. Or when Visa decided to reframe itself from being a financial services company to a digital company. This changed everything not only at the customer level but at the back office and corporate levels. An inclusive team moves swiftly to change tempo or key, to adjust production schedules, explore alternative suppliers, develop new metrics, and reassign responsibilities and tasks all while maintaining efficiency and meeting deadlines.

Personalization

Personalization occurs when an inclusive team creates space for solo breakouts. We all love the sound of a tight band fully in flow. But we also love the thrill of different band members stepping into the limelight, lightly supported by the rest of the band. It adds variety and texture to the performance. The same goes with organizational inclusive teams. Each team member's unique skills and backgrounds, discovered through the disciplines of Connecting and Caring, offer something unique that would benefit the current project or challenge. Have a team member on a roll? Stand back and give them room to shine.

HAVING A WIN-TOGETHER MINDSET

Synchronizing requires teams to seamlessly transition between structured and spontaneous rhythms. For this to occur, a shared knowledge of the rules and expectations and a shared trust in each member and the team as a whole are necessary.

Within the discipline of **Connecting**, trust building is a foundational practice. **Synchronizing** requires trust as well, but of a different kind. The Connecting discipline is about trusting the inherent and learned capabilities of each *team member*. With the Synchronizing discipline, inclusive teams learn to trust in their *team's* ability to win together through the power of their collective intelligence.

Building this kind of team trust requires each member to put the team ahead of themselves. They must believe that the team will be more powerful and win bigger together than each member can alone.

Winning together requires sublimating one's ego for the greater good of the team win. We know how difficult this can be, particularly within organizations structured to reward individual rather than team achievement. Here's how cycling teams in Tour de France handle this paradox.

In a peloton the lead rider takes on the full wind resistance for the benefit of not just their team members, but also for the people in the teams they are competing against. But there is also reciprocity: When the lead rider uses up their strength facing the wind, another rider takes their place and the peloton keeps moving forward.

The Tour's cycling teams live the duality of individual and team glory. Most casual fans focus on who won the yellow jersey, the reward granted to a winner of any of the twenty-one stages. But the one yellow jersey winner at the end of each stage is there because their team of seven others helped them get there—even as those same team members were competing at the same time *against each other* for the yellow jersey.

As the race unfolds, radio communications make it clear who within the team is riding the strongest that day. The team applies their collective intelligence and maneuvers to provide additional advantages to their lead teammate. They can synchronously slow down the peloton, block riders from other teams from breaking away, initiate a decoy breakaway on an upward slope to tire out the other riders, or use many other tactics to keep giving their leading team member the edge. If successful, their team member's solo win also leads to glory for the whole team.

Now let's explore an example from the corporate world. Organizations with team-based reward structures can employ the same mindset as Tour de France cycling teams.

Instead of "How can I maximize my sales credit?" team members should answer the more holistic question: "What does the team need to achieve to maximize sales?" This shift in perspective triggers a divergence in decision-making. The former mindset, driven by individual gain, could hamper collaboration—no one wants to share their individual rewards. In stark contrast, the latter perspective recognizes others as invaluable assets, integral to enhancing the collective chances of success.

A self-centered strategy might yield temporary benefits. However, this short-term gain is likely to be offset as team members gradually withdraw their support. There is an inherent limitation in a purely individualistic mindset when it comes to sustained and comprehensive success.

Mind the gap.

STORYTELLING

Stories are to our spirits what breathing is to our bodies. They keep us alive. Without stories, humanity withers—and not only out of boredom. Stories connect our present to our past and shape the way for a future yet to unfold.

Never has humanity consumed more stories than we do today with our seemingly infinite number of channels and technologies. Audiobooks, print books, e-books, social media, photos, film, dance, sculptures, fashion, jewelry, cartooning, digital media . . . stories are everywhere.

Storytelling is embedded in our daily speech from the moment we rise to the time we lie down at bedtime. "What's the plan?" "How was your day?" "What happened?!" "Tell me a story."

In inclusive teams, stories take the forms of case studies, anecdotes, after-action reviews, scenario-based planning, and personas. These stories are told via words, data, and images, Venn diagrams, 2×2 tables, and bell curves. They open up our understanding of the enterprise reality. They inspire coordinated action by creating both a sense of order and revealing the possibilities of disruption.

When teams are Connecting and Caring, the focus is on each team member's stories. When teams are Synchronizing the focus is on the stories of the *team*—what has shaped it, why it exists, and what it will accomplish for the broader good of the organization, and, by extension, for its customers, clients, and even the broader society.

Team stories are unifying narratives that allow teams to understand the journey that they are on together and what they need to synchronize. They elucidate the team's common purpose, their common struggles, and ways to overcome them together. These cohesive narratives also help the team be much more effective in their outward reach to other stakeholders, other teams, and customers.

We recognize that many of you may not feel comfortable in the role of storyteller, but in a world of so much change we're here to encourage you to try new approaches to maximize the impact of your teams. Let's break it down and try out some new things.

Storytelling at the team level involves *knowing your audience, mastering storytelling techniques,* and *using different modalities.* Since much has been already written on the first and last of these, we will dive deepest into the innovative sub-practice of using different modalities.

KNOWING YOUR AUDIENCE

Coming up with a self-centered story is as easy as breathing. It takes the shape of what makes sense for *me,* what motivates *me,* what gives *me* what I need. But effective, influential storytelling is not about "me." It's about reaching *others* in ways that make sense to *them,* that motivate *them,* and that give *them* what they need. A story is only as effective as the influence it has on others.

In this way, knowing your audience relies on the inclusive team disciplines of Connecting and Caring. When we know and are considerate of who our team members are—their identities, their professional and personal life experiences, and their motivations—we can shape our team stories accordingly. The cognitive and affective empathy you nurture as you learn about your audience is the key to figuring out the story you want to share with them and how.[6]

MASTERING STORYTELLING TECHNIQUES

Not surprisingly, what makes for a great thriller, historical novel, or a bedtime story also works for good corporate context storytelling. You may recognize how we ourselves followed this approach in the many stories we have incorporated into this book. In the following sidebar we provide the basic storytelling elements as they apply to team stories.

STORYTELLING ELEMENTS

Core Message

Identify the main lesson or message that aligns with team values and goals.

Audience

Determine the target audience and customize the story to their interests (see Knowing Your Audience).

Characters and Setting

Highlight key team members and the operational setting. Bring real people into the story—from a new intern to the CEO. Portray them as humanly as possible while detailing their aspirations, struggles, and triumphs. Do so through sharing personal anecdotes or experiences that shaped their professional journeys—knowledge you've picked up through Connecting and Caring.

Narrative Structure

- Introduction: Present the team and the initial challenges it faces.

- Rising action: Outline obstacles.

- Climax: Describe a key achievement.

- Falling action: Explain how challenges were managed.

- Conclusion: Sum up the journey and outcomes.

- Call to action: Tell them the three things they need to do today, next week, this year, and in the next few years.

Engaging Elements

Use dialogue and details to vividly depict the team's environment. Paint a picture of the challenges and opportunities within the industry in a way that highlights the human aspect—the impact on the team and their organization, employees, customers, and communities. Data trends, statistical analysis, and competitor data are also powerful storytelling devices. A combination of hard data and human stories is powerful in team stories.

Emotional Elements

Convey a range of emotions to enhance relatability. Incorporate not only the commercial challenge and the opportunity but also the human dimension of people aspiring, struggling, fighting, and collaborating. Underscore the emotional stakes involved—the stress of a tight deadline, the teamwork amid uncertainty, the joy in overcoming a tough challenge. Leave the audience feeling inspired and ready to act.

USING DIFFERENT MODALITIES

Stories can be orally transmitted or written down. But they can also be visually displayed or performed. There are so many effective modalities for teams to tell the stories of the challenges they are facing, the ideas they want to explore, and the future they envision.

An innovation in our inclusive teams approach is to bring the arts into the inclusive team process as a way to activate multiple places in our individual and collective brains in order to come up with new thinking and ways of seeing what is possible as a team.

Admittedly, suggesting activities such as percussion and cartooning in the workplace might at first glance seem trivial and not relevant to the business at hand. Stay with us for a moment to learn about the science behind these concepts. We will also share some powerful outcome-based examples of these concepts in action.

Neuroscientists have observed that the prefrontal context is where our executive decision-making capabilities reside. Other parts of our brain get activated through the arts—speech, dance, and so on—creating a cerebral manifestation of teamwork.

When members of a team simultaneously activate all these areas of the brain, this is when the collective sparks of new ideas and never-thought-of-before concepts start to pop, pop, pop.

Contrast that with a brainstorming session, which is almost 100 percent a cognitive prefrontal cortex exercise. Further, such sessions are usually conducted in boxes: rectangular meeting rooms or square Zoom boxes, rectangular whiteboards and flip charts or square Post-its. What a cognitive trap! How are we to think outside the box if we remain, literally, in boxes?

CEOs clamor for innovation. But to have innovative outcomes we must have innovative input and innovative processes. Science proves that the arts activate more parts of our brain than merely thinking, leading to more creative out-of-the-box ideas.

Here's a primer on three art forms (drumming, improv, and cartoon thinking) that can have a positive impact on team Synchronizing. And yes, whatever you do, find your way out of the quadrilaterals of the corporate world to do the work of team innovating and Synchronizing.

Drumming

Evidence of drumming as an ancient practice goes way back. Hieroglyphics of communal groups drumming in ancient Egypt date back to 3000 B.C.E. and pieces of terra-cotta percussive instruments have been found in the Indus Valley in India dating back to 3300–1300 B.C.E.

In five studies done by different researchers in different countries testing different conditions, drumming has proven to be a catalyst for synchrony.[7] There are positive effects gained from a group drumming circle: greater feelings of connectivity within the group, higher levels of cohesion and performance, elevated willingness of others to join in, and enhanced recovery for members of drug addiction support groups.

One study conducted on therapy groups notes the following:

> Drumming produces physiological, psychological, and social stimulation that enhances recovery processes. Drumming induces relaxation and produces natural pleasurable experiences, enhanced awareness of preconscious dynamics, a release of emotional trauma, and reintegration of self. Drumming addresses self-centeredness, isolation, and alienation, creating a sense of connectedness with self and others.[8]

But when it comes to drumming, it's not all about harmony and being on the same beat. Syncopation is when different rhythms are intentionally played slightly before or after the main beat. It creates unexpected twists and turns in the music, and by defying the expected beat, syncopation builds musical tension. The return to the main beat then provides a sense of release, which can be satisfying for the listener. This push-and-pull effect is an essential part of musical phrasing and dynamics. And it's easy to see the value of syncopation in inclusive and diverse team dynamics.

Yes, you want the flow and the alignment, but not the sameness through-out. Teams need the syncopation of different team members marching to their own drummer. Note that well-done syncopation does return to the main beat after the detours and the rhythmic clashes.

Improv

For corporate and organizational types steeped in best practices, proto-cols, rubrics, procedures, and processes, the concept of improv in a team setting can be unsettling. The reason why it's unsettling is the same reason why it can be so effective: Improv is about letting go.

For teams seeking to be more in sync and to generate new thinking, it's the very act of letting go that then opens new vistas and possibilities. Letting go means not knowing what comes next, and that can be a wonderful thing! Rather than falling back on the usual as one is trying to figure out the unusual, letting go of the known can open us to new possibilities.

While we think of improv as being for actors and comedians a la *Saturday Night Live*, there are five key concepts applicable to the organizational setting and that improve synchronization among teams.[9]

Say "Yes, and . . .". This foundational principle of improv involves accepting what another participant has presented ("yes") and then expanding on it ("and"). It promotes collaboration and encourages the flow of ideas without judgment.

Listen Actively. Good improvisers are excellent listeners. They pay close attention to their partners, tuning in to verbal cues, emotions, and body language. Be aware that some people, for a variety of reasons (including being neurodiverse), may not pick up on these cues. So, check in to ensure they are following and understand what is being communicated nonverbally.

Embrace Failure. Improv encourages embracing mistakes as opportunities for learning and humor. It helps build a safe environ-ment where participants feel free to take risks and be creative without fear of judgment.

Make Your Partner Look Good. The goal in improv is not to outshine others but to support them in a way that enhances overall performance. By focusing on making your partner look good, you create a positive and supportive environment that is conducive to creativity.

YES, AND?

One of our favorite improv principles for getting teams to sync up and spark creativity is "Yes, and?"

A team did a simple exercise with eight people at a round table.

The first person said, "I have an idea for a party . . ." and then explained their idea.

The next person responded with "Yes, but . . ." and filled in the blank.

This was repeated until everyone in the group had spoken. As you can imagine, by the end everyone was sitting on a pile of bummers.

They then repeated the exercise, but instead of "Yes, but . . ." each person had to say, "Yes, and . . ."

The result? Exhilaration and connection. They were all now ready to go to the fictitious party.

That team then repeated this exercise with a real-world problem: "I have a solution to our problem . . ." They all saw how it was going to go, but they nevertheless went through both rounds of the exercise. After the first round, they could all see how many instances of "Yes, but . . ." organically popped up in their daily workflow, quite consistently contributing to stagnation and disengagement with one another and their projects.

These rules have been around a long time and we were unable to locate the definitive source. We do not claim ownership of this idea and if you know the definitive source, please do let us know and we will credit them.

Stay Present. Improv requires participants to be fully present in the moment. Preplanning or dwelling on past scenes can hinder spontaneity. By staying present, improvisers can react authentically to the unfolding scene. This is an example of practicing mindfulness.

Cartoon Thinking

In his groundbreaking article, "The Science of Cartoon Thinking: Proving That Making People Laugh Can Transform the World," *New*

Yorker cartoonist Pat Byrnes writes, "It may seem funny to consider cartoons as a business tool—until we look at the science behind what they do, not only in the individual mind, but in the collective consciousness."[10]

We agree. Explaining or understanding the difficult or unexpected lies at the heart of not only a good cartoon but all innovation and culture change, particularly in human-centered areas such as ethics compliance, DE&I, policy, customer engagement, and team building. Byrnes adds, "Could the thinking, then, that goes into creating a gag or one-image cartoon benefit organizations seeking such transformations? Funny as it may sound, yes! The evidence comes from somewhere funnier still: neuroscience."

Byrnes unpacks the science behind his methodology. In a group setting within a digital tool that participants can access, he will use pre-created cartoon tropes (a shipwrecked person, a manhole cover, a corporate desk, a knight, a bear, a palm tree on a desert island) that users can drag and drop to create a scene with a punch line.

He explains that our brains contain large-scale neural networks—the *Executive Network*, the *Default Network*, and the *Salience Network*. When they are all activated and working together, they manage different thinking processes such as creativity, innovation, behavior change, and problem solving. *(For more detail on what each of these networks do, see this chapter's Neuroscience Corner.)*

"Gag cartoons are more than funny pictures," Byrnes writes.

> They also tell a story, with a beginning, middle, and end, expressed in a single "decisive moment." To get the gag, we must intuit what came before this moment and what is likely to follow. We cross-map all its informational cues with our personal knowledge and empathize with each character to discern motive and intent, and then put it together to reveal what it means. To do that quickly, the story framework must communicate quickly—instantly— as a trope, or *Metaphor*. Our connection to that Metaphor—a desert island for loneliness, Noah's Ark for organizational pressures, a boardroom for any number of corporate conflicts—produces an understanding of one thing in terms of another.

HOW CARTOON THINKING SWITCHED THE PUNCH LINE ON BUSINESS ETHICS TRAINING

Pat Byrnes

Business ethics compliance not only saves companies legal costs and damage to their reputation but is affirmatively good for business. Ethical cultures lead to higher employee satisfaction and retention, better innovation, and more productive teams—all of which happen to be attractive to customers. Companies named among the World's Most Ethical Companies "outperformed a comparable index of large cap companies by 24.6 percentage points from January 2017 to January 2022,"[11] according to Ethisphere's Ethics Index. Bottom line: Ethics compliance is a good thing.

So why do compliance officers so often feel like the bad guy around the office? That was the challenge The Drawing Board was recruited to address during the 2022 Global Ethics Conference. Our mission was to help several dozen senior compliance officers from Fortune 100 companies and other large organizations rethink their messaging around compliance issues like anti-corruption, culture, and conflicts of interest. After some introductory exercises to orient them to playful visual reframing (a.k.a. Humor + Drawing + Metaphor), we proposed that if their messaging about how to do things right was producing adverse effects, they should try doing things wrong instead.

Not literally, but in a cartoon.

They used a manipulable digital template to construct cartoon analogs of their Do It Wrong messaging. Reimagining the nature of these conflicts in nonliteral environments—a desert island, an enchanted forest, a funeral home—with the presumptive goal of encouraging mishaps succeeded in generating laughter, which lowered the emotional barrier to speaking candidly about what was behind that laughter—the "aha" in the "haha."

What they realized was that it was much easier to *feel* the consequences of bad compliance choices. Modeling them as metaphoric examples brought the underlying principles to the fore and sidestepped the legalistic parsing that so often results in rationalization. The fact that all parties shared the laughter was a welcome alternative to the resentment that typically meets lectures about rules and policies. The compliance officers welcomed the new framework that supported compliance based on compassion instead of compulsion.

The insights from this experience didn't just inform their own understanding. Ethisphere, the conference host, tapped several of them to inform cartoons to be included in its growing library of Ethitoons, which are a feature of manager tool kits for internal compliance training.

Seeing the relationships, understanding them from a different perspective, and being able to laugh about them—that's what transformative thought is about. And transforming thought—and feeling—is the key to transforming behavior. That is why, as *Ethisphere Magazine* puts it, "cartooning is such an effective method for getting people to think differently about ethics, compliance, integrity, and culture. And, how the art and craft of wielding humor as a means to bring people together can work in ways that no other form of outreach can" (see figure 6).

PULLING IT ALL TOGETHER

Imagine a team-building session—best done off the corporate campus—that features multiple layers of opportunities for synchronicity. It is a place where drum circles, storytelling, and "Yes, and . . ." exercises activate the various parts of our multifaceted brains and unlock the collective intelligence of all team members.

Business leaders obsess about not leaving anything on the table. But when it comes to underutilizing the knowledge of neuroscience to optimize the thinking and performance—the Synchronizing—of our teams, that's exactly what we are doing.

Yet for all the Synchronizing this discipline is aiming for, the team context remains ripe for misinterpretations. It's time now to explore how to leverage the most difficult of differences among us: worldviews. **Cultural Dexterity**, the fourth discipline, is next.

"Sure, bribery is a slippery slope, but not as slippery as the slopes on this all-expenses-paid ski trip."

Figure 6: Pat Byrnes & Emily Flake, 2022 (Permission granted by Pat Byrnes for print)

CHAPTER 3 SUMMARY

- Synchronizing occurs when team members are coordinated in time and purpose and where multiple elements or entities align collaboratively and harmoniously through systems, networks, and devices.

- Synchronizing requires teams to seamlessly transition between structured and spontaneous rhythms. For this to occur, a shared knowledge of the rules and expectations, and a shared trust in each member and the team as a whole, are necessary.

- Team stories are unifying narratives that allow teams to understand the journey that they are on together and what they need to synchronize. They elucidate the team's common purpose, their common struggles, and ways to overcome them together.

- Inclusive teams can employ artistic activities, such as drumming, improv, and cartoon thinking, to activate the areas of our individual and collective brains that spark new thinking and ways of seeing what is possible as a team.

SYNCHRONIZING TIPS

Embrace a compelling framework for team meetings. Assign motivating names to meetings that reflect their purpose and goals. Create a common language for the team (for example, one company called it "home day" when all team members came to the office for a series of meetings once a month). Utilize color-coding and font type in calendars to visually represent different meeting types or priorities. Use rituals such as opening reflections or team acknowledgments to build connection and momentum before diving into agenda items.

Establish and reinforce clear team norms. Define specific communication norms, such as response times for emails and messages, meeting etiquette, and preferred channels for collaboration, and align on ways team members can hold each other accountable for implementing these norms.[12] The latter may include the creation of tangible artifacts (team playbook, posters, etc.) or agreed-upon communication signals. In the French Navy, the most senior officer at a dinner table moves forward one of his "attributes"—a collection of solid-brass miniatures positioned in front of their plates at the table—to signal to other officers that they had just broken a rule of conduct, like speaking ill of someone absent or going on too long on a topic.

Have regular reciprocal feedback sessions. Weekly or monthly meetings that consist strictly of information sharing are going to move the needle on team Synchronizing. Teams require regularly scheduled interactive discussions that allow for a free flow of questions, challenges, suggestions, and recommendations to grow their shared understanding of the work and move toward greater synchrony.

Prioritize "We" over "I." Use both structural and behavioral methods to encourage practices that prioritize the collective over the individual. Structural choices may include performance management mechanisms and rewards models that encourage consultation and collaboration. Behavioral strategies may include setting up ad hoc meetings or choosing to do more asking than telling.

4

Discipline 4:
Cultural Dexterity to Integrate Diverse Perspectives

*Cuanto más entiendes la música,
más fácil puedes bailar.
(The more you understand the music, the easier you can dance.)*
—Orlando Gutiérrez Boronat,
Cuban author

PRESENT A BUSINESS CARD in Japan holding it face up with both hands? Sure. Kiss on the cheek or shake hands? Depends on the culture. Is slurping one's soup polite or not? Again, it depends. Is pointing out someone has gained weight an insult or a compliment? Hmmm.

Portions of this chapter first appeared in *The Inclusion Paradox* by Andrés T. Tapia, 2016, Korn Ferry Institute.

CULTURAL DEXTERITY

The ability of team members to discern and consider their own and others' worldviews, solve problems, make decisions, and resolve conflicts in ways that optimize cultural differences for better, longer-lasting, and more creative solutions.

■

While knowing the correct cultural protocols is an important sign of respect, the dos and don'ts above are the lowest-hanging fruit to building trust between people who are different.

What really trips teams up is that each member can have a profoundly different interpretation of another's words, facial expressions, body language, and actions. These interpretations are deeply rooted in world-views influenced by any combination of inputs: cultural and socioeconomic background; religion; geography of one's hometown; national, regional, and community traditions, habits, and rituals; and so on. No wonder a person's intent is so exceptionally vulnerable to being misread.

So many of the benefits of practicing the **Connecting**, **Caring**, and **Synchronizing** disciplines will come tumbling down if a team is not agile or skilled enough at maneuvering cultural dynamics.

Every minute, someone in the corporate world who is different from the mainstream, someone whom the corporation wants in their midst because diversity is a business imperative, is not feeling included. Others are making cultural missteps directed at them that make them feel like they don't belong. And on the other side, because they are not part of the majority population, they are acting in ways that lead to raised eyebrows, sidelong glances, and the "tsk, tsk" of "don't they have a clue?"

More than just acknowledging that we're different from one another in vital ways, we must navigate these differences to succeed together. Whether in government, academia, nonprofits, or the corporate world, never before have we seen such an intersection of powerful, competent, and ambitious talent working together on behalf of common organizational missions—but with wildly differing ways of going about it. This makes **Cultural Dexterity** a must-have for inclusive teams.

Cultural Dexterity, our fourth discipline of inclusive teams, is defined as *"the ability to discern and take into account one's own and others' values and practices, to be able to solve problems, make decisions, and resolve conflicts in ways that optimize cultural differences for better, longer-lasting, and more creative solutions."*[1]

Like building great management and leadership competence, one Cultural Dexterity classroom or online learning experience won't do the trick. It requires a systemic, continuous approach that changes underlying assumptions about managing differences, how we assess and reward people, the kind of talent we hire, the structures and processes we put in place to get things done, and how inclusive teams need to engage each other. This means that learning about and skill building around this discipline must change. Most of us would not be able to handle algebra without first learning basic arithmetic, and so it is with learning how to navigate our differences in truly inclusive ways.

First-generation diversity work led to "tolerance and sensitivity" training that taught us to be aware and accepting of others' differences. It was appropriate for that era. Handling the business card, making the greeting, slurping or not slurping the soup—this type of cultural awareness is the price of admission. But it won't get us through the whole performance.

Tolerance and sensitivity was a decent start. Tolerance is a good antidote to resistance and defensiveness on the part of majority groups and those in power toward those who are different. But it's a place of truce rather than truth, manifested in statements such as: *I won't resist you anymore. I'll tolerate that you're here. I'm okay, you're okay. We'll agree to disagree. Live and let live.* It's the answer to, *Why can't we all just get along?*

Sensitivity takes it further. It finds its voice in statements such as: *I will work at understanding that you have unique needs and preferences. When you say that something bothers you and it doesn't make sense to me, I accept that it is important to you. I won't question your views, and I won't resist them.*

Cultural Dexterity goes even further beyond *You've got yours and I've got mine.* It allows teams to rise up in a collective voice that asks: *What is ours—together? Out of our differences, what new progress can we create— together? How can we make each of our worldviews a part of how we all see the world? Can we change our approach due to what we have learned from each other so that we can perform better as a team?*

We'll break down how Cultural Dexterity allows inclusive teams to discover how they can use their differences to create something new and better together in the section. Please note: Some of the examples we share deal with the individual as opposed to the team because the work starts there—knowing oneself and then becoming more aware of one's colleagues. Eventually, however, this individual work, by its very essence, leads to team inclusion.

THE BENEFITS OF SKILL BUILDING AROUND CULTURAL DEXTERITY

Cultural Dexterity requires us to look at our cultural differences, call them out, ask deep questions about their underlying assumptions, and suspend our own cultural judgments (we all have them).

Compared to Tolerance and Sensitivity, Cultural Dexterity is:

1. **A discipline.** Cultural Dexterity requires a set of discrete, observable, and trainable skills and practices. It not just an attitude or stance.

2. **Pragmatic.** Cultural Dexterity provides a means for resolving differing worldviews.

3. **Versatile.** Given the expanding definition of diversity and the all-embracing nature of inclusion, it can be used in navigating all kinds of differences on a team, not just traditional diversity issues—for example, differences in thinking styles, functional roles, organizational cultures coming together in an M&A, and so on.

4. **Not accusatory.** No group, no matter how marginalized, has an inborn Cultural Dexterity gene. The implied audience in Cultural Dexterity is all of us. So, to the White heterosexual male feeling singled out: Yes, you need this—and so does everybody else!

5. **HR-system-compatible.** Cultural Dexterity can be presented as a set of expectations on which employees will be measured so that its connection to work, expected outcomes, and pay rewards is clear.

6. **Applicable across stakeholder groups (e.g., other teams, customers, and investors) to create better solutions.** Remember? No group has an inborn Cultural Dexterity gene.

CULTURAL DEXTERITY WITHIN INCLUSIVE TEAMS

Here's a story by Andrés on what the stumbles in the journey can look like and how to begin to master our responses.

How could I have missed it?

I really thought I had agreement from the group. After all, one of the team members had even said, "Andrés, I agree with you 100 percent." Yet when I started acting on the agreement I was sure we had, the emails and voicemails started flying in:

"Hey, what are you doing? We did not agree to this!"

Confused, I replied, "So what part of 100 percent didn't I understand?"

As a Latino in corporate America, I once again had broken some unspoken rule, missed some commonly understood signal, and a foul was called. I was yellow-carded. But unlike on the soccer field where it's clear what I did wrong, on this corporate field I had no idea. Making things even more difficult was the fact that my colleagues weren't aware I didn't know what had gone amiss.

What had gone amiss, I was to learn through much trial, error, and observation of the corporate human resources function culture I was operating within, was that I was a middle-class Latin American guy with a direct style of communication working within a White, "Midwestern-nice," feminine, indirect-communication-style environment.

What I had missed were the body language and code words signaling disagreement that people with similar cultural backgrounds intuitively interpret.

"But didn't your smiling, nodding, and taking copious notes mean that you were agreeing with me?" I exasperatedly asked.

"Ah, no, Andrés. That meant we were listening respectfully, but do not confuse that with agreement."

Which I, indeed, had done.

Conversely, other Latin Americans would have interpreted my own body language and code words correctly, but not my White colleagues.

So how did this mutual lack of Cultural Dexterity show up? At performance review time, their 360° evaluations of me were littered with devastating judgments, such as "not a team player," "does whatever he wants," "arrogant," and "rude." The gendered interpretation: "typical guy riding roughshod over the women on the team." And then the national culture interpretation: "typical caudillo attitude," in reference to my having grown up under a military dictatorship.

But since it was a 360° evaluation, I had my chance as well. My judgments of them were equally as devastating: "duplicitous," "passive aggressive," "don't mean what they say, don't say what they mean," "weak."

And so it went. They thought I was confrontational. I thought they were dishonest. They thought I was disruptive. I thought they were inefficient.

This was a terrible place to be in for a team that was seeking to nurture the conditions for a more engaged and psychologically safe culture. Here I was the first-ever chief diversity officer in the organization, charged with leading the way to a more diverse and inclusive company globally, and I was failing at inclusion with my most immediate circle of colleagues.

Diversity is not only a demographic inevitability, but it's also a requirement for innovation. Yet nurturing diverse teams that are also inclusive is not easy. Diversity is inherently more complex to manage than homogeneity. In fact, the more diverse the team, the *more* guaranteed the friction. The innovative, creative combustion of a diverse team can either lead to destructive explosions or generative bursts.

To channel the heat of the friction toward the generative, team relationships across cultural divides require a shared knowledge and understanding of cross-cultural issues *plus* a belief that we need those differences for surviving and thriving as a team.

Next, let's explore the three practices that must be mastered to pull off this challenging yet high-ROI discipline:

1. Understanding our own self-identities,

2. Being curious about others' cultural identities, and

3. Creating a shared team identity.

NEUROSCIENCE CORNER

Understanding the Influence of Culture on Our Emotions

Amelia Haynes

Our understanding of emotions is shaped by cultural norms and beliefs about emotions.

These are often transferred through language that parents and caregivers use to communicate beliefs, rules, and values about emotions. Emotion concepts and language provide information about ideal behavioral responses and coping mechanisms. Research suggests that processing emotion-related words engages neural systems like those involved in real-world emotional experiences.

Culture has an important impact not only on what we know, but also on what we think and believe about what we feel, which in turn has a direct effect on how we behave.

For example, the process of directly naming emotions can in itself trigger emotional states. Scientists discovered that words that capture categories of emotions, such as "disgust," influence how individuals from different cultures interpret facial expressions. If they were thinking of or experiencing joy, they tended to interpret a neutral facial expression as being happier than if they were thinking of or experiencing anger. This is because exposure to emotion words, including the process of naming emotional experiences in our own minds, triggers connectivity and perceptions in the brain, highlighting the role of cultural upbringing.

Culture plays a significant role in this experience because different cultures have different norms around these emotional experiences, how they regard them, and how people are expected to behave in response to them. For example, in Western cultures, shame is often considered negative and associated with withdrawal. However, in other cultures, shame is valued—it signifies propriety and helps repair relationships. These two different interpretations would trigger a series of different cognitive processes, one related to withdrawal and another related to respect, that would likely result in very different behavior from that individual.

In a team setting, it is important to understand not only how our own cultures may be influencing us, but how others' cultures may impact how they show up and why.[2]

UNDERSTANDING OUR SELF-IDENTITIES

The practice of understanding our own identity often trips people up. It seems so self-centered and ethnocentric.

"Isn't the core issue that I see things too much from my own point of view?" people challenge.

Yes, ethnocentrism—me at the center of the universe—is a challenge to practicing Cultural Dexterity. Yet we can only understand similarities and differences if we have a reference point, and that reference point is each one of us: who and what we know best (figure 7). Ultimately, Cultural Dexterity is a compare-and-contrast exercise between who we are and who others are.

At the core of the breakdown between Andrés and his colleagues was that none of them were self-aware enough to grasp the root causes of their misunderstandings. They did not have the language of direct and indirect style of communication. They were clueless that what they felt inside of them as "true" was actually relative and subjective.

"Of course, it's best to say it like it is," Andrés's gut felt. But in his colleagues' sense of what was right, the feeling was "Of course, it's best to disagree gently."

In our work we take each member of a team on a journey of self-discovery. We enable them to explore their formative experiences (based on nature and nurture, what we refer to as "born with" and "born into") where there has either been no or very little choice—it's the culture we inherited.

But there are more layers to self-identity. On top of the layer of formative identity lies the layer of "aspirational pursuits." Here, within

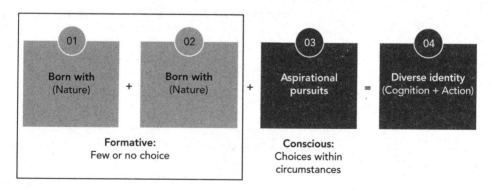

Figure 7: Your story (Korn Ferry, 2020)

circumstantial limits—we can't change the color of our skin, a disability, or the upbringing we had—we have a lot more choice about how we are going to declare to ourselves and to the world who we are. Depending on our aspirations—our career ambitions, who we want in our intimate circles, our causes and hobbies, and so on—we may choose to dial up or down our formative identities.

Acknowledging these layers shakes up the more simplistic notions of our diverse identity. What we are born with and born into are not fully determinant and fixed in terms of our adult worldviews or our ways of behaving. People can make conscious decisions about their appearance (hair, wardrobe, tattoos, workout regimes), their professional training (certifications, more degrees, public speaking), differentiators (keep or reduce or eliminate accents), memberships (clubs, boards, volunteerism), and so on. And the choices made are highly influenced by circumstances and the person's relative power within a team or organization.

We all face pressures of assimilation or threats in society that induce us to cover who we are. While some threats can be obviously destructive, many threats are often so subtle that they are not obvious to others on the team or even to us. But conversely, as we press toward authenticity, we may leverage our unique differentiators to make us more effective and powerful leaders.

A finance industry Chinese executive in Shanghai strides across the stage to take her seat for an interview in front of five hundred people. Her executive presence shows up in her power business skirt and jacket. Her differentiation: six-inch leopard-print high-heel Jimmy Choos. After a captivating segment on the hard work, courage, and determination it takes to get to the top, she's asked about confidence—especially as a woman in a male-dominant field.

She points to her shoes.

"I'm sure you noticed them," she acknowledges knowingly. "When I was in my first corporate job straight out of college, I wore flats. And since then, with every promotion, I bought new pairs of shoes each time with slightly higher heels. As you can see by now, I have had a lot of promotions. I now have the power and standing to dress as I see fit."

The executive was clear about who she was and how she wanted to present herself. But as she pursued her aspiration and kept moving forward, she gave herself increased freedom to express her identity until there was no more covering she needed to do.

Shoes, hair, and wardrobe may sound superficial, but they are far from it. They are very visible statements that people make about their identity and how they want to show up.

When confronted with this practice of understanding one's own identity, some people become paralyzed—as if there was one right answer about how they are choosing to show up in terms of their race, nationality, gender, and so on. But there is no one right answer. There is only a right question: Who am I?

Culturally dexterous team members lean into answering the questions for themselves. It is the one major individualist action within inclusive teams that is necessary to being part of a strong diverse and inclusive team.

BEING CURIOUS ABOUT OTHERS' IDENTITIES

A grounding in our own identity gives us the benchmark we need to better understand how others view the world differently due to their own born-with/born-into stories.

What people are born with, born into, and then trained in leads to beliefs and preferences about how to evaluate what is going on, how to communicate about it, and what to do about it. And in our diverse and global world today, those cultural preferences are a source of confusion and frustration in organizations.

Researchers have found that people from similar cultures often have similar beliefs and preferences influenced by their shared experiences in a country or community, for example.

Interculturalists rely on cultural dimension or cultural spectrum models to explore these preferences. The most prominent ones (popularized by Fons Trompenaars, Charles Hampden-Turner, Erin Meyer, and Geert Hofstede) present differences in terms of communication style, hierarchy, time management, and power distribution on a continuum.

Here we will draw from Trompenaars and Hampden-Turner, authors of *Riding the Waves of Culture: Understanding Diversity in Global Business*. They were puzzled by how multinationals with strong corporate cultures struggled with national differences getting in the way of being able to work as effectively as they wanted. To better understand what was going on, they created an extensive survey with a series of "What would you do?" scenarios that they deployed in different companies around the world.

Here's one: You're riding in a car with a friend who you know is speeding. Suddenly, the flashing lights of a police car appear in the rearview. After pulling the car over, the officer asks you, "Was your friend speeding?" What would you answer?

Ninety-seven percent of Swiss would say, "Yes, my friend was speeding," but only 32 percent of Venezuelans would give the same answer. What's going on?

The authors came up with seven different cultural dimensions to explain the ways people from different cultures would approach the same scenario and the impact it would have on diverse teams and organizations. In the case of the speeding car, they developed a construct that identified what individual cultures determine is fair. Some cultures believe that all rules apply to everyone equally. Trompenaars and Hampden-Turner referred to them as Universalist. Other cultures determine what is fair based on the context of the situations. These they referred to as Particularist cultures.

In returning to the case of the speeding ticket, one can now imagine the judgments flying. The Universalist turns to the Particularist and says, "How dare you lie to a police officer!" while the Venezuelan turns to the Swiss and retorts, "How dare you betray a friend!"

Both want the same thing—fairness—but they have different ways of interpreting what fairness is. In their book, the authors explain how these kinds of worldview clashes happen daily in the workplace, as workers try to figure out whom to confer status to, how to get work done, and how to manage time, projects, and emotion.[3]

See table 5 for a quick overview of Trompenaars and Hampden-Turner's Seven Cultural Dimensions.

Keep in mind that these seven dimensions work like three-dimensional chess; there are inevitable differences among individuals within the same culture or subculture, and shared preferences by different cultures on one dimension does not mean shared preferences on the other. Furthermore, these markers are relative and can only be used when comparing one culture with another. For example, mainstream American culture can seem *Neutral* to a Latin American, but highly *Affective* to White Anglophone Canadians.

A worry that often emerges when presenting cultural dimension models like this one is, "Aren't we at risk of falling into the trap of stereotypes?" So, let's make a distinction between archetypes and stereotypes.

Table 5 Hampden-Turner's Seven Cultural Dimensions

TASK	INTERPRETATION A	INTERPRETATION B
How do we define what's fair?	**Universalism** Focus on the rule	**Particularism** Focus on the specific context
How do we get things done?	**Task** Focus on the destination (outcomes)	**Relationship** Focus on the journey/quality of the relationship
How do we confer status?	**Achievement** Focus on the accomplishment	**Ascription** Focus on the title
Where do we get our sense of identity?	**Individualism** Identity comes from the self	**Collectivism** Identity comes from the group one is part of
How do we manage emotions?	**Neutral** Focus on restraint in showing emotions	**Affective** Focus on showing emotions
How do we define time?	**Sequential** Focus on one thing at a time	**Synchronous** Focus on the big picture
How do we manage our environment?	**Internal Control** Focus on dominating the environment	**External Control** Focus on accepting whatever comes
How do we most effectively communicate?	**Direct-style Communication** Prioritize saying it like it is	**Indirect-style Communication** Prioritize helping others save face by hinting at the issue

(Trompenaars and Hampden-Turner, 1989)

An archetype is the tendency of a group of people to behave in a certain way. Cultural dimension models categorize cultures by archetypes. A stereotype is the belief that *all* members in a cultural group behave according to the archetype for that group. For example, people from Latin America are more likely to be less rigid about time compared to Germans. But this does not mean all people from Latin America are less rigid about time, or all people from Germany are rigid about it.

TWO DIRECTORS AT ODDS

Julie (not her real name) was on an upward career trajectory in a prestigious global luxury organization in Paris. She had a string of very successful assignments as a marketing director in different parts of the world.

Then she began to stumble when she started reporting to Vikram, a charismatic, successful expatriate executive from India. And the ensuing friction spilled over into making the team uncomfortable.

As a French leader, Julie was accustomed to what she called a "refined and sophisticated" approach to business, deeply rooted in Gaelic aesthetic traditions: eloquent communication, meticulous planning, and an emphasis on individual accomplishments. In contrast, Vikram's leadership style was deeply rooted in the collectivist principles of his Indian heritage. His emphasis on teamwork and consensus building challenged Julie's autonomy in decision-making. This led to misunderstandings and misinterpretations, leaving Julie perplexed and frustrated and the team atmosphere tense and uncertain.

Julie sought the help of an Indian colleague in Mumbai in whom she could confide to help her better understand Vikram's ways. One early insight he offered was that she and Vikram were on opposite sides of the direct-indirect communications spectrum. Julie, now more self-aware that hers was a direct style and more other-aware that Vikram's was a more indirect one, began incorporating more collaborative language in her exchanges with Vikram.

Not only did her working relationship with Vikram improve, but the change in her communications approach marked a turning point in Julie's leadership style. She realized that blending her French creative drive with his Indian sense of inclusive teamwork could yield new, breakthrough ideas for marketing campaigns. Vikram's openness to feedback and encouragement of diverse perspectives also fostered a collaborative environment that surpassed the sum of its parts. Not only did dynamics improve between the two, but they also improved team spirit.

These positive team dynamics are what then leads to the third practice of Cultural Dexterity: creating a shared team identity.

CREATING A SHARED TEAM IDENTITY

It is in this third practice that teams experience the payoff of the discipline of Cultural Dexterity. Here is where much of the groundwork can be leveraged to optimize the team members' many differences for strategic advantage and optimal performance.

Several years ago, Tyronne and Susan worked on the same diversity and inclusion team at a global consulting company. They are different from each other in many ways. Tyronne is an African American man from Detroit and Susan is a biracial White/Indigenous (Oneida) woman from Las Vegas. Beyond that, the differences only get magnified.

Both were responsible for operationalizing strategies, though in different spheres of responsibility. Susan was very task-oriented, while Tyronne was very relationship-oriented.

Their team-project-related interactions sounded something like this:

MANAGER: Hey, Susan and Tyronne, I have an idea for a new strategic initiative. I want to get your thoughts on whether we can get it done by mid-June.

Susan would then start to immediately sketch out the tasks, sub-tasks, and sub-sub-tasks. She would figure out how many days each one would take, factoring in holidays, workloads, slippage, vacations, and the *probability* of sick days. Then, Susan would map out the timeline, along with project details.

SUSAN: I know that you want it mid-June, but because of these other issues, I'll need an extra two weeks. So, let's plan on the first week of July for a final completion date.

Contrast Susan's response with Tyronne's.
Tyronne would start immediately brainstorming aloud.

TYRONNE: I know so-and-so is going to be in town at a conference . . . maybe I can bring him in. I don't know anybody in this other area, but I know someone who knows someone in that department. I know that you want to have this done by mid-June, but if we plan on doing it early in July, we can piggyback on another conference when one of the speakers will already be in town.

They arrived at the same end date but approached it in an entirely different way. Having both Tyronne's and Susan's widely divergent approaches—and allowing the entire team to lean into these differences versus bucking them and having team members back into their corners— broadened and deepened the group's reach and impact.

Given these two disparate approaches, Tyronne and Susan sometimes drove each other a little crazy.

Both were very effective, but their processes differed in nuanced and major ways. They operated on completely different systems. Susan's

---

PARADOX: CULTURAL DEXTERITY CAN LEAD TO CULTURAL RELATIVISM (ANYTHING GOES)!

Learn more in chapter 6.

———■———

---

anxiety rose when she didn't see a written plan. Tyronne's anxiety rose when he didn't see a list of the right people to draw into the process. Tyronne's cell phone was his baton for directing his project orchestra. Susan's project plan was hers. Each made music in his or her own way.

You bet it wasn't easy. Mismatches and mutual judging of those who are different contribute to the underlying tensions between people within a team and make inclusion more elusive. It also contributes to the phenomenon of higher turnover among those from nondominant cultures. Employees who are different from the norm often are assessed as poor performers at worst or just not top-notch talent at best. Depending on the dominant culture of the organization, they may be seen as too abrasive or too passive, too controlling or too submissive, too standoffish or too friendly. On and on the judgments go, and teams fail to leverage their diversity inclusively.

Tyronne and Susan had to lean in hard to make their differences work for them or risk undoing the team. The waters were rough, and the team needed to expertly navigate the rapids through the myriad rocks and bends. Table 6 shows the harmonic and discordant notes of their styles as they worked together.

Once they grasped that they had different means but were working toward the same objectives, the judgments fell away. Their mutual appreciation for their differentiated approaches increased as they realized that together they had more tools in their tool kit to face the many challenges and opportunities in the workplace. As a team, their new shared identity became one of getting things done with practicality and flair.

BACK TO ANDRÉS

And how did Andrés end up resolving his breakdowns with his colleagues?

Table 6 Tyronne and Susan's different ways of working

WORK STYLE	TYRONNE	SUSAN
Focus is on getting the job done through	Relationships	Tasks
Mantra	Seize the day!	Plan ahead!
Highest priority	Front stage	Back stage
Leads work team's symphony with	His cell phone	Her project plan
Shortcuts	Know the right people	Cut back scope
Sounds the alarm	We don't know the right people!	We don't have enough time or resources!
Source of anxiety in working with the other	Her structure	His spontaneity
Source of learning in working with the other #1	Her structure	His spontaneity
Source of learning in working with the other #2	Leverage project tools to structure fluid working relationships	Leverage relationships to lubricate sticky tasks

(The Inclusion Paradox by Andrés Tapia, 2015)

It was about applying the principles here. We took a step back and fostered awareness of our differences. We learned about the cultural dimensions and that there was no right or wrong way, but there were differences and that those differences had names. Direct and indirect communication. Prioritizing tasks versus prioritizing relationships. The Trompenaars stuff.

This helped my colleagues and me see ourselves as benchmarks to each other's differences and similarities and, without judgment, begin to figure out whether it was best for me to adapt to someone else's way, for them to adapt to my way, or for us to create a new team norm that was a combination approach.

Creating this team norm required deliberate and explicit conversation to arrive at this alignment. That's the power of inclusive teams in creating a shared identity. Not only in who the team is but how the team wants to operate inclusively with each member of the team participating. Once we did this, we spent a lot less time judging and instead getting productive work done.

NARROWING THE CULTURAL COMMUNICATION GAP BETWEEN GENERATIONS

by Chloe Carr

Generational diversity poses an additional cross-cultural challenge to teams seeking to be inclusive.

Younger generations have been reinventing language forever. With five generations now in the workplace, the invention of new slang, which is now occurring at the speed of the internet, is the source of much confusion and misunderstanding.

Let's compare the two generations on either end of the range—Gen Z (anyone in their twenties) and Baby Boomers (those sixty and older)—and explore how the Cultural Dexterity practices of understanding one's own identity, being curious about others' cultural identities, and creating a shared team identity play out.

Terms like "herding cats," "KPIs," and "core competency" are as commonplace as accidental reply-alls and pre-meeting small talk. But to talent new to the workforce, this jargon may sound like gibberish. In fact, LinkedIn and Duolingo surveyed over eight thousand professionals across eight countries and found that 58 percent feel corporate vernacular is overused among their coworkers. Scroll through any one of the major apps, and you're bound to see Gen Zs poking fun at "bland" corporate-speak.

On the other hand, Gen Z's expressions like "smh," "ofc," and "IYKYK" may be just as confusing and even seem unprofessional to their managers and colleagues. Baby Boomers' laments about not understanding their "entitled coworkers" abound.

It is no wonder, then, that 60 percent of workers surveyed by LinkedIn and Duolingo say they have to figure out jargon all on their own and that the process causes stress and slows productivity.[4]

Overcoming this communication divide is possible, however. Here are four ways to bridge the gap.

(continued)

NARROWING THE CULTURAL COMMUNICATION GAP BETWEEN GENERATIONS

(continued)

1. **Use plain speech instead of relying on buzzwords, cliches, or slang.** Instead of "Let's leverage our core competencies to create a win-win situation for all stakeholders," how about "Let's use our strengths to make a good deal for everyone involved." Likewise, instead of writing "idk, this project is lowkey sus, ngl," how about, "I don't know. I don't trust what's going on with this project, to be honest."

2. **Adapt your communication styles.** Millennial employees often prefer texting, emailing, or chatting over phone calls or meetings because they find these methods faster and more expedient.[5] Furthermore, because Gen Z grew up online, its members tend to use emojis, gifs, and memes to express themselves. Instead of dismissing these methods as inappropriate, their older colleagues should try to understand and appreciate their benefits. Of course, Gen Z employees are not off the hook. They should be willing to adjust their communication style as well. This could mean knowing when to use formal or informal language, when to be concise or detailed, and when to be in serious mode.

3. **Learn from your differences and use them to your advantage.** As more companies permanently shift to hybrid and fully remote structures, leaders can learn from their younger employees about how to stay connected without being in the same place.

4. **Have fun with your differences.** Yes, language and our interactions with one another are enriched by new slang and terminology, but be aware that your favorite ways of saying things may not be understood. Instead of judging others for not "getting it," adapt your approach as suggested earlier *and* in a friendly, inviting way, introduce and explain your lingo.

The communication divide between Gen Z and Boomers and others in the workplace is not insurmountable. Additionally, work is not the place for extremely casual language or confusing, outdated jargon. All generations must practice Cultural Dexterity so they can better understand, respect, accommodate, and collaborate with each other.

In the end, it's not enough to tolerate differences or learn more about them. In the upside-down, 24/7 world of today, to be successful means "I need your differences. And you need mine."

PULLING IT ALL TOGETHER

As a segue from the discipline of Cultural Dexterity to the next and final discipline, **Powersharing**, here we introduce a cultural dimension that speaks directly to different views of power: low versus high power distance. Geert Hofstede posited that low-power-distance cultures are comfortable with a more egalitarian approach in interactions between people of different levels. Meanwhile, high-power-distance cultures are influenced by hierarchy: who interacts with whom and how. But don't confuse power distance with how decisions are made. Some cultures prefer top-down decision-making and others prefer to make decisions by consensus. Some cultures also seek harmony as a top priority, while others see confrontation as the best way to get results.

The following scenario shows the impact of different power distance and decision-making preferences among team members.[6]

PART 1: CULTURAL TENSIONS AND MISUNDERSTANDINGS
Context

Unity Software, an emerging tech firm, has brought together a team that is comanaged by four individuals from different cultural backgrounds and with equal organizational status:

- Raj from India (archetypically from a culture with high power distance, top-down decision-making),
- Yukio from Japan (high power distance, harmony, consensus decision-making),
- John from the United States (low power distance, top-down decision-making), and
- Anika from the Netherlands (low power distance, direct communication style, consensus decision-making).

They have been asked to develop a new collaboration tool but face challenges on how to organize themselves due to their differing approaches to power distance, authority, and decision-making as products of their cultural backgrounds.

The First Meeting: Setting Expectations

Anika (Netherlands): Let's not default to a top-down approach. I propose we share leadership equally.

Raj (India): An interesting idea, but having a clear hierarchy has always streamlined decision-making in my experience.

Yukio (Japan): I believe Anika's suggestion has merit. We should ensure everyone feels included in the process.

John (USA): Sure, but without a decisive leader, aren't we risking inefficiency? We need to move quickly on this project.

The Cultural Standoff: Increasing Frustrations, Deadlock, and Disappointment

Raj: We seem to be going in circles. Anika, your "shared leadership" isn't getting us anywhere fast.

Anika: I thought this would foster collaboration, but we're just stuck. Yukio, how does this usually work for you?

Yukio: Well, we value consensus, but this indecision is counterproductive. Perhaps we underestimated the need for clear roles.

John: Everyone is too polite to take charge. This is going nowhere. We're already behind schedule!

Anika: This is frustrating. We're all trying to be respectful, but it's leading to paralysis.

Yukio: In trying to avoid stepping on toes, we're tripping over ourselves. We need a more structured approach, perhaps.

Raj: I've been waiting for someone to take the lead. In India, I'm used to respecting the hierarchy, and I didn't want to overstep.

John: And I didn't want to bulldoze anyone with the "American way." I thought we were going for a more democratic process here.

PART 2: THE PATH TO A CULTURALLY AGILE SOLUTION
The Epiphany: Seeking a Better Way

Yukio: Let's take a step back. Our diversity is a strength, not a weakness. We need a system that reflects that.

John: I agree with Yukio. We have to leverage our cultural strengths instead of letting them divide us.

Anika: Okay, let's draft a plan that allows us all to contribute our best. Maybe rotating leadership can work after all.

Raj: Rotating leadership could work, but we need clear guidelines on how we make decisions within that structure.

Building a Framework: Iterative Adjustments

Anika: Let's define the scope of decision-making for the leader of the month. They can make operational decisions but strategic ones should be discussed.

Raj: That's a start. We should also have a system for raising concerns that can be addressed by the group.

John: I'll set up a simple traffic light system in our project management tool. Green for go, yellow for caution, red for full stop and discuss.

Yukio: I like it. This visual cue will help us navigate our discussions and respect each other's perspectives.

Refining the Process: Adaptation and Mutual Respect

Raj: The traffic light system is working, but we're hesitating on yellow issues. Let's tackle them head-on in our weekly meetings.

Anika:	Agreed. And let's celebrate small wins to keep morale high. It's important we acknowledge our progress.
John:	I'll start a "kudos" channel in our communication tool. A place for shout-outs and positive feedback.
Yukio:	Excellent. Recognition of efforts will enhance our team spirit. Let's also share constructive feedback privately to foster improvement.

UNPACKING THE DYNAMIC

As you read the scenario you can see the initial stances each protagonist takes based on their archetypical cultural preference. For example, it's not surprising that Anika from the Netherlands would be the first to speak given that Dutch culture is known for its low power distance, consensus-driven approach, and comfort with mentioning the difficult. Because of this, her character was likely to initiate discussions naming what could be awkward and suggest shared leadership and collaborative approaches.

In the end, this inclusive team finds ways to challenge each other, brings forth their best thinking influenced by their diversity, and cedes to different perspectives to achieve what the whole team is accountable for to achieve together. Ceding doesn't always happen this easily, however, as we will explore next with Powersharing.

CHAPTER 4 SUMMARY

- Cultural Dexterity goes beyond having tolerance and sensitivity.

- Cultural Dexterity is the ability to discern and take into account one's own and others' worldviews to solve problems, make decisions, and resolve conflicts in ways that optimize cultural differences for better, longer-lasting, and more creative solutions.

- Cultural Dexterity requires understanding your own identity, being curious about others' cultural norms and identities, and creating a shared team identity.

- Archetypes are the tendency of a group of people to behave in a certain way. Stereotypes are the belief that all members of a cultural group behave in a certain way.

- Different worldviews, values, and preferred ways of doing things will create tensions. Taking a step back to not judge but rather understand how the different styles can contribute to a project's development will increase the chances of team success.

- Regardless of differences, a team must agree to a set of team norms to function effectively and succeed.

CULTURAL DEXTERITY TIPS

Diversify your news sources. Expand your horizons by reading news from various international publications to gain insights into different markets, societal and economic trends, and geopolitical developments. The following reputable sources publish in English or have English-language editions: *The Financial Times* (UK), *Le Monde* (France), *The Economist*, *EuroNews*, *Mail & Guardian* (South Africa), *Daily Nation* (Kenya), *Mexico News Daily*, *The Japan Times*, *Hindustan Times* (India), *Folha de S.Paulo* (Brazil, click on the English edition option), *Buenos Aires Times* (Argentina), *South China Morning Post* (Hong Kong), *China Daily* (Mainland China), *The Jakarta Post* (Indonesia), and *The Straits Times* (Singapore).

Employ the cultural buddy system. Reach out to a team member from a different cultural background and become "cultural buddies" by exploring each other's worlds in the context of work or in more social situations. Consider attending cultural events together. Ask each other questions about what growing up was like in your culture of origin: Who was their hero and why? What did they find most difficult to adapt to when experiencing another culture?

Put together an inclusive recipe book. Compile a team recipe book—not for food, but for successful cross-cultural interactions. Each team member contributes a "recipe" with ingredients like active listening, adaptability, and cultural humility. Include the ways in which each person, in their own words, reflects or not the norms of their own culture. The recipe book will become a valuable resource for building effective relationships across cultural boundaries.

As a team, set time aside at an offsite to engage in a "storytelling circle" exercise. One by one, allow team members to share cross-cultural experiences—a travel memory, a delightful cultural misunderstanding, a heartwarming connection, or something they learned through a cross-cultural relationship locally or through a movie or book. As each person shares, all team members should actively listen and practice empathy.

5

Discipline 5: *Powersharing* to Ensure Equitable Contributions

There is no delight in owning anything unshared.
—Seneca, Roman philosopher
and playwright

A RESTAURANT KITCHEN AT PEAK TIME is a team space in seamless choreographed synchronicity. Vital to this surge of energy is the full-fledged Powersharing flowing throughout the clattering of pans and pots, the shooting flames, and the constant flow of water throughout the room.

While there can often be too many cooks in the kitchen, there can sometimes be not enough chefs. While most of us think of *the* Chef, a

POWERSHARING

The ability to unleash the power of each team member equitably to yield the best and most creative results.

---

typical high-end restaurant kitchen may have ten chefs,[1] all of whom yield power over their domain and yet must cede power to their teammates to accommodate the end-to-end flow of preparing multicourse meals for an onslaught of customers.

At the heart of a culinary team is the *sous chef*, the executive chef's right-hand person. The sous chef position demands meticulous precision and the ability to orchestrate the seamless execution of myriad tasks. The role extends beyond mere execution of orders; it involves coordination of the kitchen, managing the timing of dishes, and maintaining the overall rhythm of culinary flow. The sous chef's power is not wielded autocratically; rather, it is shared judiciously to optimize efficiency and precision. It requires entrusting authority—that is, sharing their power—to others in the kitchen with specialized skills, such as the *pâtissier* or pastry chef.

The *pâtissier* contributes their own unique set of skills to the culinary symphony of the kitchen. With an emphasis on artistic flair and imaginative finesse, the pastry chef introduces a creative dimension to the team. They also share power over their culinary works of art. They collaborate with the *executive chef* to ensure the dessert offerings complement the overall menu in terms of flavor, texture, and presentation; they coordinate with the *sous chef* and partner with *line cooks* on dishes that require the use of different cooking stations (for example, a hot-from-the-oven baked confection paired with ice cream). During service the pastry chef works closely with the service staff to ensure timely and accurate delivery of desserts. All these interactions and handoffs require clear communication and quick adjustments to meet specific guest requests or dietary needs.

What happens in organizational teams is comparable to what's taking place in these kitchens. While they are not cooking up meals, inclusive teams are cooking up plans and executing them. Each team member must pull their own weight, bring to bear their unique expertise, and share power. In other words, they must work together, taking the lead *and* stepping back as necessary to ensure progress toward a common goal.

THE COUNTERINTUITIVE NATURE OF POWERSHARING

The word *power* can be triggering.

We recognize that many people have experienced power in the hands of others negatively—in the form of abusive relationships, unfair treatment at work, and discrimination in society. At a large scale, the misuse of power leads to oppressive regimes, wars, and civil strife. At a more intermediate scale the abuse of power in the work environment leads to a host of bad scenarios like hostility, harassment, disrespect, psychological put-downs, and toxic relationships that, predictably, lead to poor team outcomes.

Before diving deeper into Power*sharing* we must first address this legacy.

The history of humankind is full of examples of the impact of power—Joseph Stalin, Adolf Hitler, and Idi Amin levels of repression and ethnic cleansing on the one hand and Scandinavian, Costa Rican, and Iroquois Confederacy levels of democracy, freedom of speech, and egalitarianism on the other. In the world of labor, history has been marked by the inhumane wielding of power over others in the form of slavery, indentured servitude, sweatshops, migrant labor exploitation, and unequal pay and opportunities for advancement, but also by humane developments such as work-week hours limits, weekends off, paid vacations, benefits, and parental leave.

Traditional power is usually exercised in a "power over" understanding where the one with power possesses control, authority, and influence over others. There will always be a place for "power over" dynamics. Ultimate authority must reside somewhere so individuals, corporations, and governing entities can make things happen. How to yield "power over" fairly, humanely, and effectively is a worthy topic to address, but that's not what we seek to explore here.

What we seek in the context of inclusive teams is a "power with" mindset and skill set. We want inclusive teams to have the power to collaborate with others. We also want individual team members to have the power to act when they have a special capability that is needed and others don't. When there is a "power with" dynamic, it allows people the power to act, even when they don't have "power over" authority to tell others what to do.

Exploitative power is the opposite of Powersharing, with those who have power hoarding and lording it over others. In such societies or organizations, a concept akin to inclusive teams would not be comprehensible. The concept of Powersharing would be dangerous at worst, naïve at best. But at the heart of both exploitive and affirming approaches toward power are values and decisions about its use. As with atomic energy and AI, human power is neutral. Its potential for conflict, creation, or collaboration resides in the willful choice of how to use it. This is why at its essence, we define power as *having the capability to do what one intends to do.*

POWERSHARING WITHIN AN INCLUSIVE TEAM

In the groundbreaking book *The Wisdom of Teams: Creating the High-Performance Organization,* Jon Katzenbach and Douglas Smith make the case that corporations must shift the traditional paradigm of individual performance and hierarchy to one focused on team performance and collaboration. While they do not use the term *Powersharing,* their tenets of mutual accountability, collective decision-making, and team member empowerment speak to this concept. That this book was written over thirty years ago, and that only now a critical mass of organizations are recognizing and acting on the power of team-based performance, illustrates how difficult this paradigm shift is to make.

Other research has added to the case for distributed power because of its outcomes of better decision-making, greater resilience, and greater job satisfaction and engagement among the company's talent.

Researchers Frank De Wit, Lindred Greer, and Karen Jehn,[2] known for their research on group dynamics and conflict within teams, concluded that Powersharing leads to better-informed decisions due to collective problem solving that involves constructive debate, the challenging of assumptions, and the critical evaluation of alternatives. In other words, Powersharing reduces the likelihood of biased or myopic choices, resulting in decisions that are more comprehensive and well rounded.

Powersharing also fortifies team resilience in the face of challenges. Steve Kozlowski and Bradford Bell, writing in their research paper "Work Groups and Teams in Organizations," explained how it creates a climate of mutual trust and cooperation, which facilitates open communication and collaboration—foundational elements for teams to adaptability and navigating change. This in turn leads to greater team agility in leveraging each member's *individual* expertise to address the unforeseen circumstances *cohesively as a team*.[3]

Embracing Powersharing within teams also fosters a workplace environment in which individuals feel a genuine sense of ownership and involvement, thereby significantly elevating job satisfaction and engagement. And this leads to business impact. According to Gallup's State of the Global Workplace: 2022 Report, "highly engaged business units achieve a 10% difference in customer ratings and an 18% difference in sales."[4]

Next we will dive into the Powersharing practices that ensure equitable contribution:

- Undoing Power Hoarding
- Turn Taking
- Addressing the Organizational Culture

UNDOING POWER HOARDING

A power hoarder is the opposite of an inclusive leader or team member. To undo power hoarding, teams need to address both behavioral inclusion (how power hoarders act) and structural inclusion (the organization's systems that can promote Powersharing).

ADDRESSING BEHAVIORAL INCLUSION

To break the back of power hoarding, we can use different approaches for different types of power hoarders.

Some power hoarders may be clueless that's what they are doing. They simply see themselves as leading in the best way they know how, which is to be the ultimate authority, the one that has the last word. Many leaders fall into this style of leadership not out of selfishness or ego but because it's how their society's or organization's cultures have shaped them to understand being a leader.

NEUROSCIENCE CORNER

Redistributing Power in One-on-One Relationships

Amelia Haynes

In times when tensions may be running high between team members, often induced by power struggles, *dyadic* sessions (guided one-on-one conversations) are among the most effective strategies in reducing cortisol and stress while at the same time increasing prosociality (behaviors that benefit others), connectedness, and altruism.[5]

Using empathetic listening guidelines in these dyadic sessions, information and experiences are shared in turn as a mechanism to build and promote trust and a positive relationship.

Research has proven that activity in the brain regions involved in empathy and perspective-taking promotes *neuroplasticity*—the ability of the brain to reorganize itself by forming new neural connections that create more positive default feelings toward those we have been in conflict with.[6]

Dyadic Protocol: Questions for Reducing Cortisol and Increasing Empathy Introduction Phase

1. *What brought you here today?*

2. *How are you really feeling right now?*

Connection-Building Phase

3. *Can you share a moment from your past week that was particularly challenging for you?*

4. *What has been a significant moment of relief or happiness for you recently?*

Deepening Understanding Phase

5. *When you face stress or challenges, what's something you wish others understood about you?*

6. *What can someone do to make you feel really supported when you're feeling down?*

Empathy Expansion Phase

7. *Have you ever felt misunderstood? Can you share that experience with me?*

8. *What is one thing you feel very passionate about? Why is it important to you?*

Reflection Phase

9. *How has this conversation made you feel?*

10. *Is there something you learned about me today that surprised you or changed your perspective?*

Closing Phase

11. *What can I do to support you after our conversation today?*

Source: ChatGPT 4.0

There are, however, power hoarders within a team who are not clueless about what they are doing. They like having power and they don't want others to have it. Let's start with this most difficult type. Influencing them to break their power hoarding habits is more likely if you frame Powersharing as looking out for the organization's well-being.

Talk to them about:

- **Resource maximization**. Stress that Powersharing is about leveraging all available talents, which improves output tactically, strategically, and motivationally. Ask them: Do you want to be part of a team where only a couple of team members are at 100 percent rather than all of them?
- **Winning**. Connect their competitive nature to the advantages of Powersharing. Better results, more innovation, and savvier risk mitigation require a culture that encourages respectful challenge from various smart, skilled team members with the freedom to speak up.
- **Legacy**. Focus on the visionary legacy a Powersharing and inclusive team can leave on the organization. Explain how Powersharing is key to driving the organization to the forefront of the industry even as it elevates the leader and their team(s) to industry leadership.

And for those *not* wrapped in ego but who simply have a more hierarchical worldview, try this approach instead. Note how the center of gravity is what is best for the team, a line of persuasion that may be particularly effective in collectivist cultures.

Talk to them about:

- **Cultivating high-performing teams**. Powersharing catalyzes team performance and innovation, with diverse perspectives leading to superior problem solving, increased creativity, and an agile response to market changes.
- **Fostering engagement and organizational health**. Emphasize how empowering team members bolsters engagement, reduces turnover, prevents burnout, and distributes risks, resulting in a healthier, more resilient organization.
- **Leadership development and legacy**. Stress the significance of succession planning and the personal legacy of leaders who leave a positive, lasting impact by nurturing future leaders and promoting a culture of trust.
- **Transformative inclusive leadership**. Illustrate how shared power is not just a leadership strategy but a transformational force that fosters inclusive behavior, builds trust, and shapes a collaborative organizational culture.

Whatever their motivation, it's essential for team members to be curious about and understand the concerns of the power hoarder, such as fears about loss of control or uncertainty about their role. Directly addressing these concerns while highlighting the benefits of Powersharing will create a more compelling case for change.

ADDRESSING STRUCTURAL INCLUSION

How an organization is structured and how teams and individuals are recognized, rewarded, and promoted can play a huge role in

---

PARADOX: POWERSHARING CAN RESULT IN ANARCHY!

Learn more in chapter 6.

■

---

promoting or hindering Powersharing. Listed here are some common approaches to making Powersharing more systemic through the adoption of processes that make Powersharing more embedded in ways of working.

- **360-degree feedback.** A traditional 360-degree feedback process involves collecting feedback from an individual's team members, direct reports, bosses, and even external stakeholders so that the individual can gain a better understanding of how they are seen throughout the organization. By incorporating diverse viewpoints, 360-degree feedback promotes a more holistic understanding of an individual's strengths, weaknesses, and contributions within a team. It also encourages team members, particularly the power hoarders, to recognize and appreciate diverse skills and perspectives.

- **Appreciation and possibilities feedback.** This differentiated approach allows everyone involved to see and benefit from the feedback in an individual's 360, but it requires certain safeguards. Perhaps the feedback is collected and shared only among teammates, for example. Perhaps the focus is narrowed to appreciations of each team member's contributions and paired with "I wonder" statements about each member's potential, leaving out any references to friction with other team members. Appreciation and possibilities feedback encourages team members to recognize and leverage diverse skills and perspectives. For example, an introverted member may end up receiving positive feedback from colleagues on their thoughtful contributions during collaborative discussions—the type of recognition that can often be overlooked in a traditional 360 feedback model.

- **Reciprocal mentoring.** Unlike traditional mentoring, where knowledge and guidance flow from senior to junior members, reciprocal mentoring allows for two-way knowledge exchange. Typically, younger employees share insights on technological advancements, social trends, and contemporary perspectives, while older mentees offer wisdom, experience, and institutional knowledge. This approach fosters a Powersharing and collaborative learning environment where both parties benefit from the other's perspectives and skill sets.

- **Anonymous straw polling**. Straw polls are conducted to test the people's opinions on a matter—a candidate, decision, or project, for example. Anonymous straw polls allow team members to honestly express their opinions on a matter without the risk of standing out from other team members. This inclusivity is vital for fostering a team culture where every employee feels empowered to contribute, irrespective of their position within the team. Further, anonymous polls are a powerful instrument for illuminating power imbalances within organizations.

- **Observational analysis**. Unlike surveys that rely on self-reported data and 360-degree feedback that involves soliciting input from others, observational analysis involves direct observation of team members' behaviors, interactions, and performance in real-world situations. This can be done by rotating team members, internal organizational effectiveness practitioners, or third-party resources such as external consultants. Having a clearly established observation framework and instruments will help consistently capture nuances and nonverbal cues that might be missed in surveys or 360-degree feedback. It will also provide a more holistic and real-time understanding of team dynamics—informal hierarchies, communication patterns, and potential sources of conflict—rather than having to wait weeks for results.

TURN TAKING

Turn taking is a practice taught in every family in every culture. It starts with parents saying a word and waiting for their infants to repeat it. Like the call-and-response flow of our drumming circle example in the Synchronizing chapter, turn-taking maturity grows as a child learns how to carry on a full back-and-forth conversation.

Yet in organizational teams, inclusive turn taking—people reacting to verbal and nonverbal cues on when to speak, when to listen, when to break in, and when to prompt others to weigh in so that all team members have a chance for equitable contribution—is poorly executed. Failures are even more pronounced when team members are from different cultures.

Why is this practice of turn taking so difficult to achieve? One reason is willful power hoarding, which we addressed in the previous practice. The other reasons are poor listening and cultural misunderstandings.

Poor listening, research has found, is often based on people being more focused on what they want to say and how they feel than on truly listening to the other person. People mistake listening as a passive "be silent" behavior, but it is actually an active "paying attention" behavior that comprises not just words but also all the nonverbal signals.[7] We discussed the value of active listening in the chapters on Connecting and Caring. Now we can see why it is also critical to the discipline of Powersharing.

Overlapping talk and silence can mean opposite things in different cultures. In some cultures, it's seen as a sign of enthusiasm and engagement, while in others, it is viewed as interruptive or impolite. The same is true with how turns are distributed, how transitions are signaled, or how long the average gap is between turns. It's not standard! In a globalized and culturally diverse environment, effective turn taking requires protocols that respect and adapt to different cultural norms. In other words, for us to be inclusive turn takers and power sharers requires the complementary discipline of Cultural Dexterity.

Note the turn-taking laments in table 7 that are common in different parts of the world. These are generalizations for large geographic footprints, but they can be indicative of how the turn-taking rules differ as well as the frustrations they can cause even within culturally similar groups when the rules are not followed. Once you've read each column and picked up on the dilemmas, imagine now a team with members that are reflective from each of the five columns. (*We recognize we don't have true parallelism by addressing cultural elements at a broad cultural level for all the columns except for the first one.*)

ADDRESSING THE ORGANIZATIONAL CULTURE

An organization's culture is the final and biggest determinant of whether Powersharing can thrive within its physical and virtual walls. Not only are current systems and processes deeply embedded, but they also shape how every part of the organization feels they need to operate.

The first step is evaluating where the traditional layers of authority are fostering power hoarding rather than Powersharing. For example, organizations with a strict hierarchy can have excessive managerial levels

Table 7 Powersharing dilemmas by culture

USA	ASIA	LATIN AMERICA	AFRICA	MIDDLE EAST
I can't get a word in edgewise. (Let's bring more innovative ideas to the project.)	Sometimes it seems like only the seniors are allowed to talk.	Everyone talks at once and it's hard to follow.	Meetings tend to be dominated by a few outspoken individuals.	Let's add more spice.
Please let me finish.	I'm not sure when it's appropriate for me to add my input.	The bosses always speak first and most, leaving little room for the others.	It's hard to get a chance to speak when there's no structured turn taking.	The tree is bearing fruit. (Our efforts will yield results soon.)
We keep talking over each other. (We must navigate the challenges ahead of us.)	It feels like our meetings are monologues from top management.	Sometimes it feels as if only the strong opinions are heard.	People speak all at once, and it becomes chaotic.	We need to find our way through the desert.
I feel like I'm being steamrolled. (Let's start with a solid foundation.)	People often stay silent even if they have something to say.	Debates sometimes become too passionate and disorganized.	In our meetings, it's more about who speaks the loudest.	A house isn't built from the top down.

(Korn Ferry, 2024)

and many leader-sounding titles, therefore creating fiefdoms in competition with each other. These factors can lead to cultures of power hoarding—as well as information and resource hoarding—the very opposite of the cross-functional dynamics inclusive teams need to optimize organizational performance.

Organizations that have been successful at changing the cultural script have had to make very difficult decisions. One key approach in high-hierarchy companies is reducing the number of supervisory and leadership organizational levels like the Bayer CEO did in the story we shared in the book's introduction. Consolidating decision-making responsibilities allows the culture to begin to shift because there is now more white space in which a greater number of employees and teams can maneuver without running into organizational boundaries.

IS IT MY TURN YET?

In any cross-cultural situation we are at the disadvantage of not knowing what we don't know—such as when it's our turn to speak. In his April 2023 LinkedIn article, "Whose Turn Is It Anyway? Turn-taking in Multicultural Meetings," organizational architect David Trickey offered the following considerations to help you decide when it's appropriate to speak and how to go about it in a culturally adept way.

Ask yourself:

- If someone should speak, who should it be?

- When I speak, how long should my turn be?

- Is there a special way that things should be opened?

- Should people speak jointly in an overlapping way or is this unacceptable?

- How should I signal that I am about to finish what I'm saying?

- How should I indicate that I would like to come in and take a turn?

- What's the best way of giving a turn to a specific person to talk next?

- If someone takes my turn from me before I've finished, what should I do?

- What's the best way of structuring the final turn that will close the event?

■

More white space empowers employees at various levels to contribute directly to strategic initiatives and to more easily create more diverse-by-design teams and collaborate cross-functionally with other teams. This approach not only enhances the flow of communication but also ensures decision-making is informed by a range of perspectives. Executive leaders can further encourage these behaviors by rewarding collaboration.

A law firm we recently partnered with reaped the benefits of Power-sharing when it made the bold move to challenge its partner-centric

NEUROSCIENCE CORNER

Perceptions of Status Can Lead to Pain or Pleasure

Amelia Haynes

Workplace practices, the structure of organizations, the style and format of performance reviews, and even small, commonplace interactions can have significant impact on whether individuals perceive their status as elevated or challenged.

The perception of an elevation in status activates the striatum, increasing dopamine levels in the brain. It triggers the same cascade of neurological activity as does receiving money or winning a competition. Conversely, the perception of status reduction is associated with the same neurological processes as physical pain.

Flatter organization structures and Powersharing practices may reduce the extent to which status is implicit and ingrained in social dynamics. However, status still functions as an internalized construct. For example, an individual may pride themselves on their internalized status of being smart or a leader (whether appointed or assumed). Status refers as much to the internalized qualities and characteristics we hold as self-truths as it does formalized rank.

governance model. In one of its leading regional offices, it invited senior attorneys to officially join the regional leadership team. Although the team size quadrupled, it facilitated a more transparent flow of information and greater diversity of views to inform team decisions.

Zappos, the online shoe retailer, embraced a radical shift by adopting a *holacracy*—a system that replaces traditional hierarchies with a more fluid, decentralized structure. This shift removed structural hurdles to Powersharing by enabling employees at all levels to contribute to decision-making. This innovative approach empowers employees, fosters a culture of shared responsibility, and exemplifies the removal of structural impediments to Powersharing.[8]

This means that in this system, teams don't have to wait for their organizations to take some elements of structural inclusion into their own hands. They can establish group norms for how they're going to inclusively communicate with each other, use the various digital collaboration tools at their disposal, and make group decisions.

POWERSHARING IN M&A INTEGRATION

Seventy to ninety percent of mergers and acquisitions (M&A) fail to reach their promised financial outcomes. One of the top reasons: lack of cultural and systems integration. Alternatively, Powersharing allows for the creation of inclusive teams with representatives from both organizations to

- address cultural differences,

- bridge cultural gaps,

- align values,

- leverage collective and diverse expertise,

- engage in collaborative decision-making,

- shape a new and inclusive strategy, and

- create buy-in and accountability.

Powersharing is particularly critical in retaining and engaging key talent after the deal is closed. Involving employees from both organizations in integration strategies and structural changes reduces uncertainty and fosters a sense of ownership in the new entity.

POWERSHARING THROUGH THE LENS OF CULTURE

Organizational culture shifts around Powersharing are made more complex by how much the cultures we come from have different attitudes, values, perspectives, and interpretations around the use of power. These worldview differences must be addressed to make Powersharing viable in teams in different cultures.

We recognize that this discipline of Powersharing is culturally influenced by our own inclusive values, in part rooted in having lived in more partici-patory systems: France, Spain (Michel), and Perú (Andrés). Nevertheless, our research and experience propel us to make the case that a Powersharing team can indeed yield the best and more creative results. This leaves us with the responsibility of ensuring cultural worldview differences are addressed to make Powersharing viable in teams in different cultures.

Borrowing from the end of the chapter on Cultural Dexterity, let's draw from well-known interculturalist Geert Hofstede, who popularized the cultural dimension of power distance.[9]

Power distance refers to the *extent to which less powerful members of a society accept and expect an unequal distribution of power*. In cultures with a high Power Distance Index (PDI), there is a greater acceptance of hierarchical order, centralized authority, and a clear distinction between those in power and subordinates. In those societies Powersharing is limited, and decisions are concentrated in the hands of a few. Authority is seldom questioned. In fact, non-leaders are conditioned to not even want to be put on the spot for their opinion and would rather defer to the leader. High power distance also affects cultural artifacts such as dress code, where people will dress more formally, and etiquette, where people are more likely to address leaders by their title or honorific (Mr. President, Ms. Chancellor, Mr. Suzuki, *Señora* Ramirez) or a generic deferential (Yes, boss, *Si, señor*).

In contrast, low-PDI cultures emphasize equality, decentralized authority, and a more consultative approach to decision-making. These cultures are more likely to embrace Powersharing, distributing decision-making authority across various levels of the hierarchy, and inclusive collaboration. Employees on teams don't hesitate to question and challenge each other and even their team leader or a higher-up executive because the ethos is one of shared accountabilities and the mutual leveraging for everyone's expertise. Culturally in the organization, the work dress code tends to be more relaxed and even the CEO may be addressed by their first name ("Call me Frank").

Another cultural complexity with engaging teams on Powersharing is the individualism-collectivism cultural dimension, which both Trompenaars and Hofstede include in their models. In individualistic societies, individuals prioritize personal interests over group interests, and in collectivist societies, it's the other way around.

Individualistic cultures emphasize personal autonomy, individual achievement, and competition. In these cultures, Powersharing may manifest as decentralized decision-making, with individuals expecting a degree of autonomy and control over their work or personal lives.

Collectivistic cultures prioritize group harmony, loyalty, and cooperation. Powersharing in these cultures often involves consensus building, with decisions made collectively to maintain group cohesion.

Understanding these cultural dimensions can help organizations, policy makers, and individuals navigate the complexities of Powersharing across diverse cultural contexts. It emphasizes the need for adaptive approaches that recognize and respect the cultural values inherent in each society, ultimately contributing to more effective and harmonious Power-sharing dynamics in a globalized world.

PULLING IT ALL TOGETHER

From an organizational perspective, Powersharing *is* powerful—and the forces arrayed against this discipline, whether consciously or uncon-sciously, are powerful as well. Of the 5 Disciplines of Inclusive Leaders, Powersharing is the most difficult to achieve given how much societal, organizational, and interpersonal corruption there has been around the concept of power. But the power of Powersharing is too loaded with octane to leave it untouched. When that is the case, it means teams are choosing to perform below their capabilities.

Interestingly, something else that leads to the substandard performance of inclusive teams is the overuse of each of the 5 Disciplines. We'll explain more in the next chapter on Paradoxes.

CHAPTER 5 SUMMARY

- Powersharing is the ability to unlock the power of each team member equitably to yield the best and most creative results.

- Power hoarding can be addressed via behavioral inclusion (for example, by encouraging leadership legacy or resource maximization) and structural inclusion (via 360-degree feedback or reciprocal mentoring).

- The practice of turn taking is key to Powersharing. In a culturally diverse environment, effective turn taking requires protocols that respect and adapt to different cultural norms.

- An organization's culture is the biggest determinant of whether Powersharing can thrive within its physical and virtual walls. Not only are current systems and processes deeply embedded, but they also shape how every part of the organization feels they need to operate.

- Organizations with a low PDI are more likely to embrace Powersharing because there's an emphasis on equality, autonomy, and collaboration.

- Powersharing can manifest itself in different ways depending on the culture. For example, individualistic cultures share power via autonomy while collectivistic cultures share power via consensus building.

POWERSHARING TIPS

Define shared and individual accountabilities as a team. As a team, identify common goals and objectives and then outline which responsibilities are best tackled together and which are suited for individual ownership. Foster open communication to ensure everyone understands their role and contribution toward shared outcomes. Regularly review and adjust accountabilities as needed to maintain alignment with evolving team dynamics and priorities. This way teams can optimize collaboration, minimize duplication of efforts, and maximize productivity toward achieving collective success.

Exercise topic leadership. Designate each individual as a "topic leader" and allow them to take turns in leading meetings, spearheading projects, driving initiatives, or designing and facilitating segments of a team's offsite.

Run a speedback session. This is a dynamic feedback experience in which team members exchange quick, focused messages to each other through a rotating process. Team members pair up to give each other feedback for about three minutes, focusing on strengths and areas for development. Rotating pairs allow each team member to both give and receive feedback, ensuring a diverse range of perspectives and insights. This process fosters open communication and a more even playing field for all team members.

6

Paradoxes to Be Navigated, Not Resolved

No mud, no lotus.

—Thich Nhat Hanh, Vietnamese
Buddhist monk, peace activist,
and author

IT SHOULD BE CLEAR BY NOW that the 5 Disciplines of Inclusive Teams do not operate in isolation from one another. Rather, they build on each other and, along the way, surface creative tensions and trade-offs. This is why teams should consider them as a system, with synergies and paradoxes that emerge as they seek to optimize each discipline.

Teams today face more unprecedented paradoxes than ever before. They must seek innovative disruption of the status quo without derailing day-to-day operations. They must foster the unique diversity of each person while nurturing the inclusion of all. Team leaders must be their team's North Star while allowing enough space and autonomy to unlock its collective power. And on it goes.

In this short chapter, we will look at the paradoxes inherent in each discipline and across the disciplines and how to navigate them. In addition, we will do a deeper dive into the paradoxical role of the leader in a self-empowered inclusive team.

CONNECTING CAN LEAD TO EXCLUSIONARY CLIQUES

There is a fine line between working toward a strongly connected team and over-connecting. When teams become too interconnected, individuals may unintentionally form exclusive cliques. These cliques often develop when a subset of team members share similar backgrounds, interests, or personalities, creating an insular environment that can alienate others within or outside the team. Within these tight-knit circles, communication may become exclusive, with information flowing only among clique members, leading to a breakdown in transparency and trust within the broader team. To be clear, we do not disparage the human reality of individuals within a team who will, for any number of reasons, have a greater affinity to specific other team members. We don't want to discourage bikers, musicians, fashionistas, anime fans, World Cup devotees, foodies, and so forth from pursuing those passions together. Inclusive teams also find a way to honor the unique interests of the subsets. The problem lies when cliques form without first pursuing team connectivity.

Moreover, over-connecting within teams can inadvertently foster a competitive atmosphere in an organization across multiple teams. As team identity solidifies, members may prioritize their team's interests over those of other teams or of the organization, leading to internal rivalries and power struggles. This competitive mindset can hinder collaboration and innovation, as individuals focus more on outperforming their fellow teams rather than working together toward common goals.

We also see over-connected teams at risk of becoming overly resistant to change or new ideas from outside sources. The insular nature of cliques will sometimes create a sense of complacency, where team members are reluctant to seek input or feedback from other departments or individuals within the organization. This lack of diversity in perspectives can stifle creativity and hinder the team's ability to adapt to evolving challenges and opportunities.

Navigation: Organizations should encourage cross-functional collaboration, promote diversity in team composition, and provide opportunities for interdepartmental communication that can help break down silos and prevent the formation of cliques. By promoting openness, transparency, and a shared sense of purpose, organizations can ensure that teams remain connected without succumbing to the pitfalls of cliquish behavior.

CARING CAN LEAD TO A LOWER FOCUS ON RESULTS

When team members overly prioritize maintaining harmony and avoiding conflict, they may shy away from holding individuals accountable, which can lead to team complacency around achieving results. Instead of addressing issues directly, they may opt to ignore or downplay problems to preserve harmony within the team.

Too much Caring can also contribute to a sense of entitlement among team members. When individuals perceive that their colleagues or leaders are overly lenient or forgiving, they may come to expect special treatment or exemptions from accountability. A lack of accountability can result in a decline in standards and performance, as individuals may not feel compelled to meet expectations or strive for excellence. A sense of entitlement can also breed resentment and undermine morale within the team, as those who feel unfairly burdened by the consequences of their actions may become disillusioned with the team's values and principles.

Navigation: Leaders must set clear expectations for performance and behavior, hold individuals *and* teams accountable for their actions, and provide constructive feedback and support when needed. Team members must ensure that Caring is expressed in ways that align with organizational objectives and values. Remember, the discipline of Caring doesn't require liking or special treatment. At a work team level, Caring is extended to others for utilitarian reasons such as shared commitment to the team's purpose and wanting all team members to feel valued and motivated to perform at their best.

SYNCHRONY REQUIRES
A DEGREE OF ASYNCHRONY

No surprise, we tend to synchronize better with people like us—biologically, experientially, educationally, and personality-wise. It's so much easier to find a common groove within an in-group. But to establish synchrony within a team with many differences, we must leave space for those differences to shine.

However, under the pressure of leaders keen on unity and alignment there can be an overemphasis on synchrony's common by-products—standardization and coordination. If team members prioritize consensus over innovative thinking, if they are quashing dissenting voices and inhibiting the exploration of diverse perspectives, then they are yielding to complacency and opening the door to exclusion of different voices. By inadvertently stifling individual creativity, teams can end up neglecting the potential benefits of adopting novel approaches. This is why teams must leave room for a degree of *a*synchrony within the group.

Encouraging constructive dissent, cultivating psychological safety, and embracing diversity of thought are crucial steps to harnessing the power of synchrony while nurturing individual creativity and resilience in the face of uncertainty.

> *Navigation*: Achieving a delicate balance between synchrony and asynchrony and between alignment and autonomy becomes paramount. Team leaders must navigate this balance by encouraging diverse opinions and fostering an inclusive environment. One way to do this is through structural methods to avoid groupthink, such as building counterfactual thinking opportunities into meeting agendas.

CULTURAL DEXTERITY CAN LEAD
TO CULTURAL RELATIVISM (ANYTHING GOES)

Respecting and working on others' worldviews no matter how different they are from our own does carry some risks. One of them is an "anything goes" mindset (also known as *cultural relativism*).

When cultural relativism leads to moral and ethical relativism, the pursuit of universally accepted ethical principles and stated corporate norms is at stake. A belief that all cultural practices are equally valid may lead to a passivity or indifference about culturally different behaviors that cross the line of globally established standards, such as those having to do with how women or those in the minority are treated.

Cultural relativism can also get in the way of the establishment of group norms. For example, if a team member from a specific culture consistently falls short of expectations, an overly relativistic approach might prevent the team from addressing the issue ("that's just how they do things in their culture"), resulting in a decline in overall team effectiveness and morale.

> *Navigation*: The antidote to cultural relativism is for the team to establish clear performance expectations and have a mutual understanding of the team's accountabilities. Plus, the regular execution of the practices within each of the 5 Disciplines of Inclusive Teams goes a long way in managing the paradox of "there is more than one way to do, think, and talk" on the one hand, and "we've got to move forward together in synchronicity" on the other.

POWERSHARING CAN RESULT IN ANARCHY

Seeking extensive Powersharing may seem forward-thinking and equitable. However, when this principle is pushed too far, it can result in detrimental effects within teams such as prolonged deliberations, indecisiveness, and a notable breakdown in decision-making structures. As every choice undergoes exhaustive scrutiny and consensus-seeking, essential tasks may languish unresolved or face significant delays and decision-making processes become chaotic and counterproductive.

Rather than fostering a collaborative environment, excessive Powersharing can stifle productivity and innovation, hindering the team's ability to achieve its goals. Symptoms of this overemphasis on Powersharing may include a lack of clear leadership direction, blurred accountability, and a pervasive sense of ambiguity regarding responsibilities. Paradoxically, in such environments, individuals or factions may vie for power without regard for the broader goals or interests of the collective. This can lead to fierce power struggles where competing factions seek to assert dominance and undermine each other's influence, creating a state of constant tension and instability. Unguided Powersharing can also result in a diffusion of responsibility and accountability. Without clear lines of authority or decision-making processes, it becomes challenging to hold individuals or groups accountable for their actions or the consequences of their decisions. It can also exacerbate existing inequalities and injustices within the organization.

Teams should be particularly attentive to the following observable clues:

- Meetings excessively running over,
- Instances of double work,
- "Power conflicts" over who has final say,
- Ballooning size of teams, sub-teams, and committees, and
- Finger-pointing and blaming.

Recognizing these clues and symptoms is crucial for teams to recalibrate their approach and restore balance to their decision-making processes.

> *Navigation*: Unguided Powersharing often occurs when there is a lack of clear mechanisms for allocating and regulating authority within a team. *Who owns the decision?* Therefore, teams must establish clear frameworks and processes for allocating, regulating, and exercising power. This may involve defining roles and responsibilities, establishing shared decision-making procedures, and promoting transparency and accountability. As we have seen for the other paradoxes, fostering a culture of collaboration, trust, and mutual respect serves as the foundation to prevent or solve power struggles and promote constructive dialogue and cooperation.

OVERALL STRATEGIES TO MANAGE PARADOXES

Teams can adopt several universal strategies to navigate the paradoxes that emerge in practicing the 5 Disciplines.

Integrate and synthesize. Approach the paradox as an opportunity for greater integration and synthesis. Teams should allocate time to find common ground or overarching principles that can reconcile the apparent contradictions under a new conceptual frame. By identifying shared values or higher-level objectives, it becomes possible for teams to create a more comprehensive and concordant understanding of the decisions they need to make.

Embrace balance. Adopt a strategy of dynamic balancing, recognizing that certain situations may require a continual adjustment or balancing act between opposing forces. Rather than seeking a permanent resolution, teams can put their attention on adapting to changing circumstances and finding equilibrium in the face of conflicting demands.

Remix perspectives. Embrace a mindset of reframing and perspective shifting. Sometimes, paradoxes arise from limited viewpoints or cognitive biases. By examining the situation from different angles and considering alternative perspectives, individuals or teams can gain a more nuanced understanding that helps reconcile apparent contradictions. Teams can also open up their meetings to external stakeholders, whether they are colleagues from other divisions or geographies or individuals from outside the organization (for example, consultants, suppliers, and clients) in order to surface different perspectives.

Imagine the impossible. Encourage creative thinking and innovation to transcend paradoxes. Explore novel solutions that challenge traditional assumptions or binary thinking. Often, breakthroughs occur when individuals or teams are willing to think outside conventional boundaries and consider unconventional approaches that address paradoxes in unexpected ways. Sometimes, this can be achieved by taking the team outside of its everyday context to work as an intact team on a completely disconnected topic, which nonetheless offers opportunities to refresh their problem-solving mindset and skills.

THE ROLE OF THE TEAM LEADER

Throughout our elaboration of the 5 Disciplines of Inclusive Teams, the paradigm shift we have been presenting is that it's *the team* that collectively owns the success of the team rather than the full weight falling on the shoulders of the team leader. Yet there's still a vital role for the inclusive team leader to play. We'll touch on it here and go into more detail in chapter 9.

Team leaders have unique accountability as stewards of team culture wielding considerable influence on how the team comes together. Since the full answer of what it takes to be an inclusive leader is already captured in the first book of the trilogy, here we highlight just a few elements from the Inclusive Leader Model that are particularly relevant to their role within more self-directed inclusive teams.

Navigation: To unlock the collective power of the team, inclusive leaders must cocreate with the team a vivid and inclusive vision of the future. Strong leadership in this context results not only in a team that is aligned on its overarching goals but also genuinely inspired by them.

When Alain became the new leader of a cross-functional software development team at a global management consulting firm, the situation was dire. The team struggled to meet the demands of their internal clients over several quarters. Alain was an external hire who came with an explicit mandate from the business to turn things around.

Alain recognized that the path to transformation had to start with building a greater sense of connection and synchrony—both within the team and between the team and their clients. But first, he felt it was important to frame for the team why these two disciplines mattered now and why they held the greatest promise for transformation.

Although the team was dispersed globally, it had a strong center of gravity in India, with 75 percent of the workforce located in the firm's Mumbai office. We helped Alain set up his first team meeting, an in-person session in Mumbai with his entire extended leadership team of fifteen people. First on the agenda was time for each team member to present who they were personally and professionally (Connecting). Then they conducted a mapping exercise to identify any interdependencies on the team and the line of sight to their clients' needs (Synchronizing). What the session surfaced, though, was the need to also address Cultural Dexterity. The exercise revealed cultural misunderstandings between the teams in Mumbai and their colleagues in France and the United States. When Alain closed the meeting, he shared his off-the-cuff observations, distilled in a few compelling statements, which helped the group leave the event with greater clarity about who they were as a team. He also got vulnerable, sharing with them how this experience had transformed his perspective and what he would start doing differently the next day. His transparency inspired the team to emulate him and find their own opportunities for renewal.

Alain's leadership impact came from his ability to frame the team's challenge: come together to drive the results their clients were demanding. It also came from his vulnerability and willingness to walk the talk alongside the team. In doing so, he helped the team synchronize on what

HOW INCLUSIVE TEAM LEADERS SUPPORT INCLUSION WITHIN THEIR TEAMS

- *Champion collaboration.* Effective team leaders ensure that every team member not only contributes but also has a substantive voice in the envisioning, developing, and decision-making processes.

- *Develop team talent.* Team leaders must see themselves as individuals and team coaches rather than directive leaders. In inclusive teams they coach and develop team members to tap into the diversity of everyone's experiences and perspectives to achieve results, and they reinforce a team mentality with team recognition and rewards. Only then can the ways in which the different individuals contribute in the service of the communal effort be called out and celebrated.

- *Build a sense of community.* Team leaders make it clear that each member is an integral part of something larger than themselves. They help keep the team's common purpose top of mind and ensure members support one another in achieving it.

- *Value differences.* Team leaders encourage team members to view cultural differences as strengths and as resources that can contribute to innovation and problem solving. To help team members better grasp this, they can create a cultural exchange workshop inclusive of self-assessment tools and introspective exercises where team members can reflect on their own cultural values, communication styles, and work preferences.

- *Balance stakeholders and manage conflict.* There will be times when teams hit a stalemate due to not enough consensus or interpersonal conflict roiling the waters. This is one of the key reasons why a designated team leader is needed: to help resolve conflicts between parties and keep the team cohesive and on track when members are at odds.

For more on the role of leaders in this new age of self-directed, inclusive teams please see chapter 9.

■

deserved their collective attention going forward and the ways in which they could work in harmony to achieve their collective goals.

PULLING IT ALL TOGETHER

A paradox is not the same as a dilemma. Dilemmas demand resolution through an either/or choice. Paradoxes demand a departure from binary thinking and an embrace of ambiguity. They require a mindset that can accept a both/and reality.

Inclusive teams don't seek to eliminate contradictions but rather manage them effectively. They acknowledge there may not be one "right" solution to a paradox and instead find ways to integrate various solutions and points of view into one.

Understanding the perspectives of all stakeholders is also key to navigating paradoxes. Inclusive teams must learn how to value different viewpoints if they want to open up to new possibilities not imagined before. Paradoxically, different perspectives open us to finding the common ground necessary to address both similar and differing needs.

Next, we wrap up part 1 by bringing together all 5 Disciplines.

CHAPTER 6 SUMMARY

- Too much Connecting can lead to exclusionary cliques.
- Too much Caring can reduce the focus on results.
- Synchronizing requires a degree of asynchrony.
- Too much Powersharing can result in anarchy.
- Too much Cultural Dexterity can lead to cultural relativism (anything goes).
- Paradoxes demand a departure from binary thinking and an embrace of ambiguity.
- To unlock the collective power of the team, inclusive leaders must cocreate with the team an inspiring and inclusive vision of the future.

7

Integration across the Five Disciplines

Wholeness is not achieved by cutting off a portion of one's being, but by integration of the contraries.

—*Carl Jung, Swiss psychiatrist and psychotherapist*

WHEN MICHEL DAMAGED HIS MENISCUS, his physical therapist's approach to healing was to focus on strengthening the muscles around his knee. Similarly, teams can improve their Synchronizing, Cultural Dexterity, and Powersharing by strengthening the foundational Connecting and Caring disciplines through the practices of curiosity, building trust, sharing a purpose, empathy, and mindfulness within those two disciplines. Some common ways that disciplines feed off each other to supercharge the collective power of teams are detailed next.

CONNECTING AND CARING

Connecting and Caring are closely linked when it comes to team dynamics. When teams build strong working relationships based on trust, understanding, and collaboration they create a positive environment for Caring attitudes and behaviors to grow.

When Connecting and Caring are activated, team members feel more emotionally invested in their team's well-being and success. This contributes to a supportive and harmonious team culture, where societal divisions based on identity can be managed and even leveraged to unlock the team's collective power.

CONNECTING AND SYNCHRONIZING

Connecting practices are the foundational tracks for greater Synchronizing within a team. In a team where members feel empowered to inquire, seek clarification, and express curiosity, a dynamic dialogue unfolds. It creates a fertile ground for increased cohesion and collaboration.

Together Connecting and Synchronizing promote a deeper understanding of tasks and objectives. When team members are committed to transparent and open communication, they create a shared knowledge base. This not only fosters trust but also ensures that everyone is on the same page regarding goals, progress, and challenges. This coordination is especially vital when the team takes on complex work with high levels of interdependence among team members. It sets teams up to tap into and benefit from the diverse perspectives and insights of individual members, a necessary condition for collective intelligence to thrive.

CARING AND CULTURAL DEXTERITY

There is a strong connection between trust, empathy, and Cultural Dexterity. Through our engagement with global teams, we have learned that individuals who take the time to comprehend, respect, and consider the values and norms of others *because* they care about each other cultivate team trust at a deeper level. This trust becomes the cornerstone for collaborations that require Cultural Dexterity and the fostering of an environment where diverse perspectives are acknowledged and embraced.

Empathy is another practice that bridges gaps and builds connections across cultures. The ability to empathize requires an authentic interest in the emotions and perspectives of individuals from different cultural backgrounds. It is the catalyst for dismantling stereotypes and fostering a genuine understanding and appreciation for the richness of diversity.

CULTURAL DEXTERITY AND POWERSHARING

Power is intimately defined by cultural constructs. Beliefs and expectations regarding the distribution, exercise, and respect for power vary significantly across cultures, influencing how diverse teams function and make decisions. Understanding and navigating these cultural differences around power is crucial for effective Powersharing.

It is common for teams that engage in Powersharing to clash over their respective beliefs about what power means. Adding on the different cultural approaches to conflict resolution can compound the issue and take the team into a tailspin. A diverse team must have the Cultural Dexterity to effectively discuss and agree on conflict resolution mechanisms that align with the preferences of its members, which in itself is a step toward Powersharing.

Feedback mechanisms are crucial for addressing organizational systems and individual behaviors that support or hinder Powersharing. Consequently, the cultural nuances surrounding giving feedback must not be overlooked. Some cultures prioritize constructive criticism, while others may prefer positive reinforcement. By openly discussing individual preferences and expectations regarding feedback, the team can develop a feedback culture that motivates and supports its members in sharing power equitably.

SYNCHRONIZING AND POWERSHARING

Powersharing without Synchronizing—and Synchronizing without Powersharing—is impossible.

Synchronizing does not happen as a top-down directive. It is by its very nature organic and intuitive, its many elements of spontaneity regulated (paradoxically, yes) by operating principles and group norms. But these are norms and principles, not rigid, inflexible rules. They are directional, intended to inform a collaborative mindset for coordinated action while leaving plenty of room for team members to bring forth their innovative and differentiated ideas in a way that contributes to the flow, even as it adds new dimensions to the collective work.

Think of a drumming circle where the invitation is always there to insert a new sound, a new counter-rhythm, or an additional percussive beat—in essence, to share the power of leading and creating. Yet those additions must preserve the sense of cohesion and common purpose, the synchrony of the sound. The other example we looked at earlier was of a peloton in the Tour de France. Different riders in different contexts take turns leading in a way that preserves the synchronicity of the group, with the result that the team becomes more effective, faster, and smarter as the race evolves.

Every project will hit its roadblocks. Every team will be threatened at some point by all kinds of external and internal factors that will require team members with different experiences and talents and mindsets to step into power in order to keep the whole endeavor clipping along in synchronicity toward its ultimate outcome.

PULLING IT ALL TOGETHER

A team of sellers and business developers in management consulting services found themselves at a crossroads. Accustomed to selling abstract consulting services—characterized by open-ended engagements, smaller financial stakes, and less residual revenue—they now faced the daunting task of selling a massive, technically complex AI platform. The contrast was stark, and their struggle palpable. This team, not yet well acquainted with each member, was thrown into a workshop to figure out how to move forward.

At the workshop, which we were called on to run, we initiated the process of Connecting. Through a set of probing questions, we facilitated a kind of sharing that had been foreign to them until now.

> *What unique experiences and training have shaped your approach to work in ways not evident from your résumé?*
> *What is something about you that we might not know but you'd like us to?*

These questions encouraged them to share aspects of their lives that directly impact how they work and what they bring to the table.

Additionally, we inquired about what they needed from us to be more authentic at work.

Next, we introduced our WeConnect model as a way to foster Caring. The model displays five taxonomies—cognitive, physical, values, societal, occupational—capturing the breadth of diversity within the group: singles and married people, parents of young and older children, educational backgrounds ranging from college to professional training, ethnicities including Latino and mixed race, personality types such as introvert and extrovert, as well as individuals with disabilities. We asked them to identify two or three elements crucial to their identity and share, as they felt comfortable, how these elements shape their self-perception and their contributions to the team.

This exercise was the beginning of building a parasympathetic interpersonal connection, enhancing trust levels and fostering a curiosity that would lead to the release of neurotransmitters such as oxytocin, elevating moods and receptivity.

The increased trust played a significant role in creating a psychologically safe space for innovation, brainstorming, and the expression of diverse thoughts that might challenge the status quo or provide alternative solutions.

BREATHING AND DRUMMING

Following, we conducted a simple breathing exercise aimed at releasing tension and preoccupations. We guided the team through mindful breathing—inhaling for a count of four, holding for four, exhaling for four—and asked them to focus on whatever was burdening them and to release it with each exhale.

After the mindfulness session, we gave each participant a pair of pencil "drumsticks" and facilitated a drumming circle to get the team in a Synchronizing space.

The drum circle master challenged the group: "How many of you think you don't have rhythm?"

As hands were raised, she countered with, "How many of you don't have a heartbeat?"

She pointed out that each heartbeat is a rhythm that keeps us alive, linking this intrinsic rhythm to the exercise. She then led the group through body movements and drumming using found objects like desks, coffee cups, staplers, paper clip holders, iPads, and Post-it notes. The starting beat was a medium-tempo bossa nova, which progressed to a faster samba beat, and culminated with an electronic dance music (EDM) tempo, encouraging free-form expression and solos.

To further synchronize the group, we introduced cartooning as a medium for collective expression. We led the team through drawing exercises, even for those with rudimentary skills, emphasizing that just as everyone has a heartbeat, everyone can draw. Even stick figures are a form of drawing!

The team members depicted their thoughts and emotions, creating cartoons featuring various characters and objects—a knight, a dragon, a bear, business people, street elements like traffic lights and manhole covers, and more—in different situations. All these situations were humorous metaphors representing the transition from selling consulting services to selling an AI platform, and the cartooning allowed the team to express how it made them feel.

We laughed at the humor in the cartoons, even as some fell flat. What became clear was the story of fear that so many of the cartoons told, a collective sentiment that we explored further. The fear was twofold: the sellers' fear of not meeting sales goals with an unfamiliar product and their perception of their clients' fear of either being left behind in the digital transformation by not moving fast enough or by making a rushed, ill-informed decision that could lead to failure.

EPIPHANY

The workshop concluded with discussions on how to sell this new technological platform and reassure clients that they would be supported with proper implementation and change management. The sellers' role evolved from *selling technology* to *selling confidence*, ensuring that all the necessary resources and expertise would be brought to bear at the right time.

The disciplines of Connecting and Caring had served as the foundation for establishing a synchronized team primed to optimize their collective intelligence. Now, the team had to apply what they had learned.

They needed to develop operational plans, update marketing materials, and continue to collaborate, honoring their differences and working together with Cultural Dexterity. They had to be okay Powersharing as needed. Much like in the drumming circle, the team needed to create the space for each person to take the lead when their specific knowledge or energy was called for.

The workshop was a microcosm, giving team members a taste of how the 5 Disciplines operate in concert.

* * *

This brings us to the end of part 1. We have unpacked what each of the 5 Disciplines of Inclusive Teams entails and the practices necessary to turn them into habits. We have explored the paradoxes of each discipline and how they work together to unlock the collective power of teams to achieve breakthrough.

In part 2 we will take a big-picture view of the implications that the new nature of teams—deconstructed, hybrid, impermanent, diverse, and inclusive—has on the future of innovation, DE&I, and leadership.

CHAPTER 7 SUMMARY

- The 5 Disciplines of Inclusive Teams don't work in isolation independent of one another. Rather, they feed off each other to supercharge the collective power of teams.

- Connecting and Caring are two halves of a circle, encircling and embracing the entirety of the 5 Disciplines approach. Everything begins with these two.

- Connecting practices are the foundational tracks for greater Synchronizing within a team. In a team where members feel empowered to inquire, seek clarification, and express curiosity, a dynamic dialogue unfolds.

- In culturally diverse teams, Power-sharing requires Cultural Dexterity to sort out cultural differences in how power is understood and used.

- Caring is the cornerstone of collaborations that require Cultural Dexterity and the fostering of an environment where diverse perspectives are acknowledged and embraced.

* * *

PART TWO

THE BREAKTHROUGH POWER OF INCLUSIVE TEAMS

What are the big-picture implications of diverse and inclusive teams unleashing their collective power?

In part 2, we lay out our vision for a bright and sustainable future driven by diverse and inclusive teams. It's time to get excited about the breakthrough impact of inclusive teams on innovation, leadership, and business outcomes.

We will also outline the steps teams, leaders, and organizations must take to create a virtuous cycle of diversity, inclusion, self-directed teams, and innovation. As we explain, it's going to require a wholesale disruption of the DE&I industry. This is a good thing!

It's time for DE&I to evolve. It's time for us to start fulfilling its long-standing promise as a catalyst for breakthrough business transformation.

■   ■   ■

8

Inclusive Teams and the Future of Innovation

I am always doing things I can't do.
That's how I get to do them.

—Pablo Picasso, Spanish painter

O N THE SHORES OF LAKE MICHIGAN, with Chicago's iconic skyline in the background, Soldier Field is pulsating to the *thump-thump-thump* bassline and scratching of Calvin Harris's headliner set at Spring Awakening, a three-day EDM festival. Rihanna's prerecorded vocals for "We Found Love" soar into the mix and the crowd of over sixty thousand enters into a collective delirium.

Innovation made EDM, once an underground movement rooted in the dance club scenes of Europe and the United States, an $11 billion global

This chapter contains content adapted from the Korn Ferry white paper, "Beyond Innovation as Usual: How and Why to Refine Your Innovation Strategy," by Michael Solomons, Alina Polonskaia, and Andrés Tapia.

mega-business that has influenced not just music but also fashion, technology, and nightlife culture.

EDM's secret sauce is its dependence on one-time and ongoing collaborations across a diversity of genres—like disco, house, techno, pop, reggaeton, dancehall, and moombahton—to stimulate artistic innovation such as the one between Harris and Rihanna. Among the many thousands of EDM DJ/pop artists collaborating to infuse pop music with electronic beats and synthesizer-driven melodies are Skrillex and Diplo with Justin Bieber in "Where Are Ü Now," David Guetta and Sia in "Titanium," and Martin Garrix and Dua Lipa in "Scared to Be Lonely."

While the DJ names will likely be less familiar for some, the pop artists they collaborate with have massive name recognition. Individuals with widely varying musical backgrounds and fan bases joining forces to blend styles, experiment with new sounds, and reach wider audiences—these ongoing cross-pollinations are how the industry continues to generate innovation and grow in relevance. Fueling the innovation within the industry is inclusive teaming—a celebration and protection of individuality while creating unity of purpose. The democratization of music production technology has also made the industry more accessible to a wider range of artists, encouraging more diverse collaborations and innovative sounds. Increasingly, collaborations are extending beyond original songs to fan remixes, social media interactions, and crowd-sourced projects, all contributing to the EDM's continued evolution.

It's global and inclusive team synchronization at 130 beats per minute.

■　　■　　■

A major flaw in the innovation field is our limiting who gets to innovate to the brilliant few. For sure, there have been iconic breakthrough innovators in science and technology such as Marie Curie, Albert Einstein, Steve Jobs, Satya Nadella, and Jack Ma. But without diminishing their astounding contributions, this stratification has reinforced the notion that innovation only sits in these rarefied echelons—ones that are often exceptionally homogenous.

In corporations, these assumptions can lead to structural exclusion with elite innovation hubs that limit who gets invited to innovate. Contrast this with the EDM industry, where innovation is distributed across technologists, dancers, vocalists, and syncopators, and from the highly renumerated artist to the ticket-buying fans.

The prevailing corporate innovator-as-God approach is not only elitist; it throttles innovation. It perpetuates the myopic perspective of a limited group of people deemed "the disruptors." It misses the bigger and more vibrant repository of innovation: *everyone else.*

Everyone else, by the way, is sitting in the structure of teams. Teams of all sizes, in all functions, in all locations.

We'll say it again: Innovation is a team sport. And teams made up of diverse players are the most innovative.

Leaders might unintentionally view diversity as a problem to be solved instead of an opportunity to be embraced. This can show up as overvaluing predictability, alignment, and detailed plans when exploring uncertainty. By minimizing variation in these areas, we send a message that any difference is bad. We must become more attuned to recognizing the true value of diversity and how to leverage differences to drive innovation (table 8).

Some organizations have long known that diverse collaboration enhances both innovation and team cohesion. For example, in today's car manufacturing companies, engineers, designers, and marketing experts coming from different industries (e.g., manufacturing and digital) now work together on new electric vehicles, learning from each other and building strong interpersonal bonds, leading to more creative solutions.

Table 8 Diversity and inclusion are enablers for growth

DIVERSITY IS A PROBLEM TO BE SOLVED	DIVERSITY AND INCLUSION IS AN ENABLER FOR GROWTH
Alignment	Product conflict
Prescriptive ways of working	Ways of working that reflect preferences and traditions
One-size-fits-all	One-size-fits-one
Outputs targets	Outcome targets
Competition—winners and losers	Cooperation
Representation as sole focus	Inclusion and equity
Counting the numbers	Making the numbers count
Plans	Options
Local optimization	System optimization
Smooth off the edges	Go to the edges

(Korn Ferry, 2022)

This is because, according to Daniel Kahneman's theory, we operate in two cognitive modes:

- System 1: Our intuitive, quick, and often unexamined mode of thinking.
- System 2: Our deliberate, analytical, and conscious mode of reasoning.[1]

Homogenous teams often find themselves operating in System 1. Familiarity within the group can inadvertently promote a shared cognitive bias, where decisions are made swiftly and assumptions are rarely challenged. These environments may breed efficiency, but they risk curtailing creativity, with innovation becoming a casualty of unexamined groupthink. On the contrary, inclusive and diverse teams provoke System 2 thinking. Here, varied backgrounds, experiences, and perspectives become a collective asset. But it does not happen automatically. It requires the diversity within the team to be activated by the team members and their team leader in a way that sparks curiosity, encourages scrutiny, and activates our slower, more deliberate System 2. This conscious mode of reasoning fosters rigorous examination of ideas and preconceptions, facilitating innovative solutions that may remain unexplored in a more homogenous environment.

Homogenized input leads to homogenized output. The permutations are limited. In contrast, with heterogenous input, the permutations are quantum.

Embracing diversity isn't just ethical—it's cognitively and commercially beneficial. It nudges us away from unthinking consensus and toward richer, more considered, and innovative problem solving. All of which, in turn, enables greater business success.

It is within diverse and inclusive teams that the future of innovation lies—all along a continuum ranging from the continual tweaks in day-to-day processes to new small- and medium-scale tools all the way to the game changers of delivery apps, smartphones, and AI. Innovation is the collective power and promise of the 5 Disciplines of Inclusive Teams. Here's how teams can put them into practice.

- Include Everyone (Including AI!)
- Create Diverse-by-Design Inclusive Teams
- Design From and For the Edge
- Build Support from Inclusive Leaders

INCLUDE EVERYONE (INCLUDING AI!)

As we all know, innovation requires challenging the status quo. But how do we do that? Answer: by involving the status quo.

Employees, the ones held accountable to maintain the status quo, are the power users of the organization. They know the drawbacks of the firm (and likely have built hacks to work around them). They know customers best. And they know when products and services delight and when they fall short.

This is why innovation efforts must include employees at all levels—and in more than just superficial or unidirectional ways (e.g., focus groups, surveys, and suggestion email boxes). Employee teams need to be heard and their ideas engaged at the deepest level. They need to be codesigners of the organization's future.

There is the assumption that a focus on innovation compromises teams' ability to get their day-to-day work done. While setting up a separate group to innovate makes a clean break between those doing the day-to-day work and those pursuing novel ways to solve problems, it derails the organization's ability to speed up and scale innovation.[2]

We must instead facilitate a team's ability to shift back and forth between day-to-day responsibilities and innovation mode through a variety of structural mechanisms, such as:

- Role descriptions that set expectations for questioning the status quo, linked to job responsibilities,
- Incentives that reward teams for collaborating outside of their official boundaries and finding better ways to solve problems,
- Policies that allow time for exploring new approaches without impacting shorter-term critical targets, and
- Collaboration tools that allow team members to dynamically network with and learn from one another.

Blurring the lines between daily execution and innovative efforts creates the necessary friction required for actionable innovation. While the skills to innovate and those to execute might be perceived as incompatible, they can be complementary (table 9). This synergy fosters what Peter Senge termed the *learning organization*—an entity that continuously adapts and grows by fostering a culture of collective learning and shared knowledge—leading to greater resilience and improved performance.[3]

Table 9 Beyond innovation as usual

EXECUTION SAYS . . . (PERFORM)	WHILE INNOVATION SAYS . . . (TRANSFORM)
Follow the mission	Follow the vision
Predictability is the goal	Uncertainty can lead to profit
Resolve the problem	Seize the opportunity
Failure results in a loss	Failure results in learning
Activities	Experiments
Answers	Questions
Process optimization	Process reimagining
Continuous improvement (10%)	Non-linear change (10x change)
Compliance	Disruption

(Korn Ferry, 2024)

Let's dig a little deeper into the differences in accountability for execution of day-to-day responsibilities (what Korn Ferry calls "Perform") and innovation ("Transform") in ways that will likely disrupt the day-to-day.

To make these contrasting areas of responsibility work in a mutually reinforcing way, teams need clear permission to experiment and learn from failures. Traditional execution models prioritize detailed planning and value certainty to minimize risks, but by not providing room for taking risks, we actually increase the risk of an enterprise being rendered irrelevant. After all, experts say that for every breakthrough innovation, two thousand ideas need to be generated.[4] Think about all those once-iconic brands that failed to innovate or even just adapt once the writing was already on the wall: Kodak, Blockbuster, Blackberry, Sears . . . the list goes on.

When teams work together to perform and transform, they greatly increase their chances of solving intractable challenges, driving growth, and capturing new markets. Research shows that organizations that manage both existing as well as new ventures had a 90 percent success rate in breakthrough innovation. This compares to a success rate of 25 percent for those that were not able to both manage their status quo and at the same time disrupt it.[5]

To democratize key aspects of the innovation process, teams can break up power hoarding in favor of *Powersharing*, as addressed in chapter 5. It starts with the team setting innovation goals instead of allowing senior executives to dictate them. It includes brainstorming sessions where members at all levels, from interns to senior engineers, contribute ideas anonymously, leading to comprehensive goals that reflect diverse perspectives. It has a rotating leadership model where a different team member acts as "project lead" each week, coordinating efforts and tracking progress in an equitable and systemic way to operationalize Powersharing. At every stage, no single person dominates the process. To support Powersharing and delivering breakthrough innovation, teams must create a safe space for questioning and learning. Encouraging open communication and continuous learning opportunities will keep the team curious and connected.

By the way, there is a new member on your team that deserves just as much attention, caring, and inclusion: your favorite AI app (though it can for sure be biased—see sidebar on the next page for how to manage).

AI is a fast learner, a data analyst, a synthesizer of information. It is also being programmed in platforms such as Microsoft's Viva as a quantitative capturer of team interactions via chats, internal social media streams, and emails that can reveal how inclusive (or not) team dynamics are. It can let us know who is power hoarding, where the team is not Synchronizing, and whether we are checking in with each other in ways that create psychological safety.

CREATE DIVERSE-BY-DESIGN INCLUSIVE TEAMS

Where can you find diversity in organizations? Answer: *Everywhere.*

Even in an organization with less visible diversity, there are people with different ways of thinking, perspectives, and insights. These show up in the diversity of personalities, specific skills, education, work experiences, and career tenures. This means that organizational groups seeking to create inclusive, diverse-by-design teams need only look around.

Seeking to bring in the more visible dimensions of diversity tied to race, ethnicity, gender, and many other forms of identity will require a more deliberate effort. For this, we recommend tapping existing employee resource groups to cocreate products and services that reflect vital and often overlooked experiences. Consider those places where a greater amount of diversity may exist—in entry-level positions, as well as in areas where this talent has been "tracked," such as in customer service, shop floors, and delivery. But we can't stop there. There are an unprecedented number of women and people of color earning college degrees in all kinds of fields, including those where they have historically been underrepresented.

Given that they represent a broader spectrum of humanity, diverse-by-design team members must be inclusive of each other for the mix to

OVERCOMING BIAS IN COLLABORATION WITH AI'S ALGORITHM

Caution: AI can show up with its own unconscious biases—that it's learned from us.

In chapter 4 on cultural agility we shared a narrative depicting cultural miscommunication and resolution among four team members from different cultures. Via interactive prompts we created that dialogue with ChatGPT.

After three prompted sequences between us and the AI engine, the dialogue produced was okay but stereotypical—too superficial and not nuanced enough.

The sequence that follows shows our real-time collaboration with, and learning on the part of, the AI:

Andrés and Michel:

Do this case study again with members from India, Japan, Netherlands, and the USA trying to figure out Powersharing as a team given they have very different worldviews about high power distance versus low power distance, and consensus versus top-down decision-making. Use conversation soundbites to tell the story. But this time tell the story with more tension and more cultural misunderstandings and a back-and-forth that reveals that misunderstandings keep happening even with good intentions on both parts. Make the characters have equal power. Also, part 1 is a dialogue just showing frustration mounting, things getting more broken down between all of them. They are all confused, and frustrated about what is going on and don't have suggestions for what to do. Then part 2 is the epiphany and resolution. But the resolutions don't happen in one back-and-forth but iteratively.

ChatGPT

[Provides a very nice script of the dialogue between the four team members].

Andrés and Michel:

Great job but we don't like it that the American is always the first to talk in every segment. Let's make someone else the first to speak. We are not sure which lead person would give us the best narrative construct and storytelling. *You* decide who that should be.

[Note that this prompt requires DE&I insight on the part of the humans. And note the "agency" we give to ChatGPT.]

ChatGPT:

[Provides a much-improved script that begins to address the deeper DE&I issues.]

Andrés and Michel:

Tell us your *rationale** for why you chose Anika to be the first to speak and then for when you switched the order of the speakers in the different scenes.

*[*We are aware AI is following a predictive algorithm and does not truly have this type of implied cognition; nevertheless, we still chose this word to see what would happen.]*

ChatGPT:

Choosing Anika from the Netherlands to be the first to speak was a deliberate decision based on several factors:

- Cultural Representation: Dutch culture is known for its low power distance and consensus-driven approach. The Dutch often favor flat organizational structures and egalitarian work environments, which means they are likely to initiate discussions about shared leadership and collaborative approaches.

- Gender Dynamics: Choosing a female voice to lead off could also subtly highlight gender dynamics in leadership and decision-making, challenging stereotypes and encouraging diversity and inclusivity in the narrative.

- Narrative Contrast: By having Anika propose a flat structure, it creates immediate contrast with the high-power-distance cultures (represented by Raj from India and Yukio from Japan), which adds tension and sets up the narrative for exploring the challenges of Powersharing in a multicultural team.

(continued)

145

OVERCOMING BIAS IN COLLABORATION WITH AI'S ALGORITHM

(continued)

For the second part, the order was switched to Yukio from Japan to show a progression in the narrative:

- Cultural Bridging: Japanese culture, while high in power distance, also places a strong emphasis on consensus and group harmony. Yukio's position allows for a shift from a discussion centered on hierarchy to one focused on unity and collaborative problem solving.

- Introducing Flexibility: The Japanese concept of *wa*, or harmony, suggests a flexibility that is conducive to finding middle ground. Having Yukio introduce the concept of stepping back and reevaluating the situation brings a sense of calm and opens the door to finding a resolution.

- Developing Story Arc: Switching the order of speakers allows for a more dynamic and engaging narrative. It prevents the story from being predictable and encourages the reader to see each character as an active contributor to the solution, rather than having a single dominant perspective.

AI as an inclusive team member? You bet.

---

work. Rather than seeking to smooth the edges of their differences, inclusive diverse-by-design teams must see those edges as possibilities for something better.

Paradoxically, one way to make this a norm is to challenge the group and organizational norms. The team can set new norms such as airing unique ideas that challenge the status quo, tapping and leveraging differences, and discussing failures openly in order to learn from them. This is where cocreation becomes a powerful ally *and* can lead to a powerful outcome: more solutions that work for more people.

The creation of a strong shared identity also helps to bring a diverse-by-design team together in a way that protects and celebrates each person's individuality. It states with empathy about wanting to learn about

FENTY BEAUTY:
A TAPESTRY OF SHADES AND TEAMWORK

by Stephanie Collins

The company Fenty Beauty, founded by pop superstar Rihanna, is known as a groundbreaking organization in the industry worth billions of dollars. But the team who launched the company to success and how they did it is not as well known.

Fenty was conceived with the notion of "Beauty for All," an innovative mission that was a big challenge to execute.

To manage the simultaneous launch of 40 foundation shades in 17 countries with shipping to 137 countries, Fenty's brand and marketing team leveraged an omnichannel approach requiring the perspective of many pro marketeers. In fact, the team brought together over 500 global leaders in a wide variety of industries, including branding, merchandising, supply chain, traditional marketing, social media, and retail, as well as a vastly diverse talent pool representing many different identity dimensions, to brainstorm creative solutions and execute with unparalleled precision. Like Olympic-level synchronized swimmers, the team worked together to coordinate and leverage their vast collective knowledge and creativity.

The team utilized a "show, not tell" approach to launch the brand. Not once did they use the words *diverse* or *inclusive*, but they fully demonstrated their commitment to these values through their products and teams. The team prioritized the dialogue Fenty Beauty had created around an inclusive product experience comprising their work and the product line.

Fenty became the biggest beauty-industry brand launch in YouTube history, was named one of *Time* magazine's best inventions of 2017, and generated over $100 million in its first forty days.

This is what a diverse-by-design team is capable of accomplishing.[6]

---

the diverse backgrounds of team members. Next, it requires collaboratively defining the team's goals, values, and vision through facilitated sessions that ensure all voices are heard. Small projects in which team members can prototype and iterate their working processes can also help refine collaboration.

Speaking of collaboration, another hallmark of effective diverse-by-design teams is an ability to distribute power equitably. As we showed in chapter 5, *Powersharing* promotes participation and empowerment and makes people more inclined to exhibit innovative behaviors, such as expressing their ideas and taking risks.[7]

DESIGN FROM AND FOR THE EDGE

A common assumption is that an efficient way to innovate is to design for those who are considered the majority. This is flawed at various levels. When designing for the majority, the number of people left out is consequentially large. Not only is it inequitable—on what basis should the needs of those not in the majority not be considered and addressed?—but it is also a faulty business decision because the service and product provider is systematically giving up on increasing its market share.

As Todd Rose, author of *The End of Average*, says, "There is no average person."

Homogenized input leads to homogenized output. The permutations are limited.

Meeting the true needs of a vast array of differentiated users is where the growth and the profitability lie.

Edge users are vital because theirs are the needs that are most overlooked in being met with products, services, and procedures. From their perch, they are also the ones with the most powerful perspective on what may be missing. They can peer into the center of the mainstream through a completely different lens that can better reveal the flaws and gaps that those in the center cannot see.

Take the case of the pulse oximeter, a life-saving medical device used to treat and monitor Covid-19 patients. It is a wonderful invention with a serious problem—it doesn't work as well on darker-skinned patients. The pulse oximeter measures the amount of oxygenated blood in a person's finger by the absorption of light into the device; however, it was not calibrated accurately to account for greater amounts of melanin in skin, leading to misreadings. For those with darker skin, these misreadings masked possibly dangerously low oxygen levels, leading to those patients being less likely to receive needed supplemental oxygen compared to their White peers. Worse yet, this outcome was known for a long time, although the underlying reason why was not.[8]

It was Black physicians who discovered the light-reading issue, one not unlike what photographers must address in adjusting lighting for different contexts (including different skin tones) or what makeup manufacturers must address in creating makeup for every skin tone. Now, with the problem identified, they are close to creating the technological solution.

Well-structured meetings with clear agendas, attendance requirements, and meeting norms are the marks of highly synchronized and therefore high-performing teams. They are also essential for designing for edge users and fostering innovation. In the consumer goods sector, companies like Unilever and LEGO have a strong legacy of focusing on edge users with specific abilities and gender-related needs. Unilever's development of the Degree Inclusive deodorant exemplifies this approach. Structured innovation sessions brought together diverse teams to focus on the needs of users with disabilities. Initial meetings centered on understanding user challenges, and teams gathered insights from individuals with limited mobility and disability advocacy groups. Detailed agendas ensured that all relevant issues were addressed comprehensively. Subsequent meetings were dedicated to prototyping and feedback. Teams presented design iterations, discussed usability test results, and incorporated real-time feedback from users. These structured discussions facilitated rapid problem solving and continuous improvements, ensuring the final product was easier to grip, open, and apply, directly addressing the users' needs.[9]

LEGO employs a similar strategy to design for edge users—in this case those with visual impairments—with its LEGO Braille Bricks. Initial meetings focused on gathering insights from educators, children with visual impairments, and organizations for the blind. Agendas were meticulously planned to cover user needs, educational goals, and potential design concepts. Prototyping sessions followed in which cross-functional teams reviewed tactile feedback and usability. Regular meetings allowed the teams to iterate quickly based on feedback from real-world testing, ensuring the braille dots were easily readable and aligned with LEGO's quality standards.

Designing for edge users requires a disciplined approach to teamwork, ensuring all members are aligned and focused. At Unilever and LEGO, a high level of synchrony allowed teams at both companies to adapt to new challenges and capitalize on emerging opportunities, driving significant breakthroughs in product development.[10]

BUILD SUPPORT FROM INCLUSIVE LEADERS

It is not enough to merely assemble inclusively led, diverse teams and expect groundbreaking ideas and breakthrough change to happen. Failing to sponsor time for employees to innovate means it won't happen. Neglecting to reward employees for their innovative efforts will result in disengagement and subpar new ideas. And if you don't equip employees in the process of innovation, their ideas may remain surface-level and overly simplistic.

Leaders have the power and responsibility to bring their teams together to combine their varied experiences and insights and sponsor their efforts. This synthesis can spark the game-changing progress that organizations strive for. It's the leaders who infuse the organization with a clear understanding of the context, emphasizing that innovation is not just beneficial but essential for growth, sustainability, and continued relevance. They weave networks, building connections among individuals and teams who might usually operate in silos. Through these networks, ideas cross-pollinate, challenges are viewed from multiple angles, and solutions emerge that might have otherwise been overlooked.

Further, leaders are the architects who build the capability within their teams. They ensure the availability of tools, time, and training, setting the stage for prototypes and mock-ups to be developed by those who may not necessarily be tech wizards. They're the champions who celebrate and reward both the process and the results of innovation. By focusing on outcomes rather than rigid predictions, they foster a culture of learning and adaptation.

Leaders also don the hat of investors, ensuring that promising ideas don't wither due to a lack of resources. They provide the funding, yes, but also mentorship, guiding fledgling ideas to become full-fledged, impactful solutions.

In the first book of the Five Inclusive Disciplines trilogy, *The 5 Disciplines of Inclusive Leaders*, we presented a full-fledged model for the various competencies and traits that inclusive leaders must exhibit. The most vital traits to innovation are *empathy, curiosity,* and an *openness to difference.*[11] In doing so, they harness the full spectrum of perspectives, experiences, and expertise within their teams, paving the way for groundbreaking innovation. *(See following sidebar for specific actions.)*

HOW INCLUSIVE LEADERS SUPPORT TEAM INNOVATION

There are five actions every inclusive leader must take for their teams:

1. **Clear the Way**—Innovation is often thwarted by barriers both seen and unseen. By proactively identifying and eliminating these obstacles, leaders ensure that their teams can operate freely and creatively. For instance, they might dismantle existing hierarchies that inhibit open dialogue or regularly review and remove bureaucratic barriers or redundant processes that can stifle creativity and slow innovation.

2. **Equip the Team**—Knowledge is power, and in the world of innovation, context is key. Leaders need to equip their teams with the tools and insights they need to succeed. This could mean connecting teams with external experts who bring fresh viewpoints and specialized knowledge to the table or allowing them to use sandboxes where they can test new technologies.

3. **Prioritize Impact**—For ideas to take root and grow, they need nurturing. Leaders must demonstrate their commitment to innovation by investing in it. This doesn't just mean monetary investments—it's about time, resources, and attention. Recognizing and celebrating those who take calculated risks, even if not always successful, can make a difference. Consider, for example, a leader who dedicates part of the budget for experimental projects or establishes an innovation space where teams can refine their groundbreaking ideas without business constraints.

4. **Create a Center of Excellence**—Leaders can create a movement that extends their impact by forming a center of excellence (COE) that helps them execute on these actions. A COE steers the organization toward sustainable, inclusive innovation by scaling best practices, setting clear performance metrics, and facilitating collaborations that break down silos. The COE may create a network of inclusive innovators who coach their teams within the flow of work. They not only champion innovation but also put structures in place to manage associated risks. Through its dedicated efforts, the COE ensures that innovation becomes a standard operating procedure, driving both growth and differentiation.

(continued)

HOW INCLUSIVE LEADERS SUPPORT TEAM INNOVATION

(continued)

5. **Be Knowledgeable and Savvy about Diversity**—Leadership that doesn't consider the reality, complexity, challenges, and synergies of diversity is akin to a car driver speeding blindfolded through an obstacle course. Dropping the blindfold means being open to and curious about the implications of all forms of diversity. Activating diversity to ignite innovation requires a versatile set of tools to influence, inspire, and coach team members who have various motivational drivers, life experiences, and cultural values.

Promoting *mindfulness* is another effective strategy for leaders to build support for innovation on the team. As we saw in chapter 2, the practice of mindfulness in teams has leaders carve out time in the team's agenda for pausing, resetting, and centering. This is a common practice we apply at Korn Ferry when creating and facilitating team development experiences, whether these occur at a team's offsite or are embedded in the team's everyday ways of working.

For example, if the team has been meeting in the same room for a couple of hours, working to solve a challenging topic, we may use a break in the agenda and take the team outside to pause, center, and reset. One pharmaceutical client Michel has worked with for many years has a beautiful pond on their property, which has served as a great setting for team members engaged in all-day team sessions to reset for fifteen minutes. When the team comes back in the room, instead of having them pick up where they left off, we may engage them in a short mindfulness exercise—a guided silent meditation or a discussion in pairs—to center before resuming their work. Considering our focus on innovation in this chapter, we recommend leaders orient any meditation exercises or discussions to a focus on what innovation means for team members at a personal level.

PULLING IT ALL TOGETHER

To thrive in the age of AI, shifting political climates, and a power-aware workforce, businesses need to perform and transform—not just in surface-level ways, but by shattering traditions deep within their cultural DNA. The key to this type of breakthrough innovation is fully activating diverse teams.

CHAPTER 8 SUMMARY

- Organizations must challenge the paradigm that innovation can only be done by a select few. They must instead find ways to unleash innovation at the team level throughout the entire organization.

- It's possible for teams to simultaneously innovate while still taking care of their day-to-day responsibilities.

- Inclusive, diverse-by-design teams have higher potential for innovative break-throughs than homogenous teams because their differences spark alternative thinking.

- Rather than kick-starting design from the center and for the center, inclusive teams should start designing from the edge for the most overlooked users.

- Inclusive leaders sponsor and reward innovation.

▨   ▧   ▨

9

Inclusive Teams and the Future of Leadership

If you want to build a ship, don't drum up the [people]
to gather wood, divide the work, and give orders.
Instead, teach them to yearn for the vast and endless sea.
—Antoine de Saint-Exupéry, French
writer and pioneering aviator

LEADERS HAVE LONG KNOWN that top-down decision-making is best used sparingly. This is especially true today in a competitive landscape that continues to shift at a vertigo-inducing pace.

Employees, customers, suppliers, and even politicians are demanding increasingly faster, simpler solutions to meet their needs and demands. At the same time, growing polarization in views and values has led to an unwillingness to compromise, and AI technology is displacing the intermediaries, go-between roles, and processes meant to ensure alignment between all parties.[1]

This level of complexity means that leaders cannot possibly do it all. Teams *need* to step up and be decision makers. They need to be self-directed. They need to take risks.

And some teams need to be the decision makers not just on day-to-day topics, but they must also give their input on the strategic direction for the long run, on charting contingency plans to get there, and on delivering the transformation outcomes.

INCLUSIVE LEADER OF TEAMS EXEMPLAR

When Barbara Melegari arrived in Melfi, in the heart of southern Italy, a region bound in traditions and old-school values, she did so as the first female plant director at Barilla's bakery.

Not only was Barbara's gender an exception to the leadership norm, but so were her visible tattoos, her status as a single woman, her Gen X worldview, and her being from northern Italy. At the welcome reception organized by an important association in Melfi, she was asked when her husband, Mr. Melegari, the assumed new Barilla plant director, would appear. Even after she corrected them, the welcoming party could not comprehend that she was the new leader.

An initial resistance to having someone like Barbara in charge of the factory manifested in many ways. But she was undeterred.

Barbara was a pioneer, the first of her kind at the factory, and she was also an accomplished supply chain leader. As part of their succession management plan, Barilla had placed her in various global roles to get her ready for the plant director position. In addition, she was used to the raised eyebrows, the mocking side glances, and the attempts at dismissal of her authority.

As a seasoned leader, Barbara knew not to make any quick judgments. Based on firsthand experiences over her years in the company and her identity as a native Italian, she was aware of the logistical, cultural, and team issues that would need to be addressed to turn around some troubling factory performance metrics. But she chose to not share those for a while.

Instead, she worked to build the trust of her direct report team. She focused on **Connecting**.

Barbara got curious about her team. She asked each person about their accomplishments and how they contributed to their team's success. She learned about the individual and collective experiences and skill sets within the teams. She asked them for their best ideas on how to address performance challenges. And she encouraged them to get curious about each other.

Trust did not come right away. It took about six months before Barbara felt ready to share her observations and insights and to trust that they would be well received. And she made sure to share them in a way that felt collaborative, not pejorative, and that led to cocreation.

First, Barbara noted how the more top-down management style of some of the tenured leaders in the Melfi factory was different from her own style of leadership and the expectations of younger team members. She opened up a discussion with them about the difference between experience and competence, which led to the creation of a reverse mentoring program that paired senior leaders with junior employees to work on various projects and to learn from each other. The connections they made allowed them to be more empathetic of each other's viewpoints and to find a new rhythm together, which ultimately led to better work products.

Next, Barbara got personal. She prioritized **Caring**.

She inquired about everyone's families, learning their spouses' and kids' names. She made it a point to ask about family members and follow up on any milestones they were celebrating. To extend Caring from within her teams to the entire organization, she encouraged everyone to use the company's internal social media site to share their successes—personal and professional—and keep up to date on the successes of their colleagues.

The internal site allowed for a new level of informality and openness for the Melfi-based workforce. And while originally the site was built to share celebratory news, it also became a place to share ideas. Teams began using the site to connect with other teams, to extend and amplify their resources, and to collaborate in new ways. When one side of the factory posted seeking help on a challenge, others in another part of the factory would share ideas, tools, and even people. She achieved **Synchronizing**.

Barbara also worked to create bridges of understanding among different groups of employees: those from southern and northern Italy, women and men, older and younger teammates. She demonstrated **Cultural Dexterity**. Barbara opened up the conversation on the impact of cultural identity by sharing her experiences as a woman living alone and having "the same job as the other women's husbands." And she encouraged others to do the same, creating a safe space for each to share important aspects of their own identities.

Last, Barbara put her collaborative leadership style to work. She practiced Powersharing. She created an organizational culture that fostered the co-ownership of ideas. She put challenges in front of the team, such as the use of social media in their workflow process, and gave them the room to figure it out together instead of simply giving them orders to follow.

Barbara created an environment in which the 5 Disciplines of Inclusive Teams could be practiced freely, and the whole factory's culture began to change. Eventually, so did their performance metrics: quality, workplace safety, efficiency, and, above all, collaboration.

Barbara used a traditional understanding of her power as leader to activate her teams to act in nontraditional ways. But she did not stop there. As an inclusive leader, her goal was to corral them into inclusive teaming. She influenced the factory's teams to own the 5 Disciplines of Inclusive Teams in ways that created more psychologically safe places throughout the factory, and this led to higher engagement scores and better business results.

■   ■   ■

Melegari's story shows how inclusive teams have disrupted the traditional role of team leaders—from top-down direction to inspiring and nurturing their teams to be self-directed; from carrying the full weight of success on their shoulders to creating an environment in which teams collectively own their success.

In inclusive teams, power begins to ebb from the hands of the one leader and instead flows throughout the team in a fluid and adaptive way that respects each member's unique abilities and background and leverages them to achieve their common goals. The team dynamically adapts to situations, with different members naturally stepping into leadership roles based on the challenge at hand, without a formal hierarchy.

But there's still a vital role for the leader to play: facilitation. Like Melegari, the leader's job becomes facilitating collaboration among team members as they organize themselves to step into their agency.

A facilitative leader helps their teams optimize their own performance by shaping the conditions for them to collectively do their best work. Such leaders serve as the catalysts for the 5 Disciplines of Inclusive Teams by:

- Coaching with Empathy
- Advocating and Empowering
- Aligning Through Storytelling

COACHING WITH EMPATHY

As we all know, with more agency comes more responsibility. As self-directed teams take on deeper ownership for outcomes, the pressure on individual team members as well as on the team collectively rises. Inevitably, tensions, rivalries, and differences surface that challenge team members' ability to connect, care, synchronize, be culturally dexterous, and share power.

This is where team leaders slide in: to provide empathetic individual and team coaching that increases trust and collaboration.

Like everyone else, leaders can get trapped in navigating the tyranny of the urgent to the point that people problems can seem like impediments to getting the work done. For inclusive leaders, coaching with empathy means they stop and consider the person in front of them and their needs. They create that trust by spending meaningful time with everyone on the team to ensure they all feel seen and valued for who they are and what they can contribute. And these leaders encourage team members to do the same with each other.

Greater empathy and trust leads to a greater willingness to own one's individual and team outcomes—and it influences teams in the direction of more effective collaboration. Through the team leader's direct coaching and indirect modeling, the team learns how to overcome interpersonal challenges and create their own path to success.

CEOs tell us frequently that collaboration is one of their most elusive goals. Stakeholders with different agendas, objectives, metrics, and personalities never fully agree on the way forward, and it takes a skilled facilitator to get all the different players to seek mutuality and collaborate toward shared goals.

The key here for inclusive leaders is to recognize that collaboration does not mean arriving at full agreement. It means getting to a place where all players care so much about their shared purpose and the cohesion of their team that they are willing to move forward together. Whether all team members fully agree with, "get," or even like each other is secondary. Empathetic individual and team coaching nudges teams in the direction of collaboration by communicating that each person is an integral part of something larger and that they are there to support one another in achieving it.

We have seen leaders achieve great success by making empathy an explicit expectation of all team members—through its inclusion in the team's stated norms, "success profiles" for specific roles or leadership levels, the leadership competency model, or the organization's values. To bring things home, they use recognition and reward to celebrate individuals for their work in service of the collective effort, and in this way reinforce the vital role collaboration plays in breakthrough outcomes. By holding themselves and others explicitly accountable for empathetic coaching, team leaders can help shift the culture of the team, and, in the long run, the culture of the organization.

This is what worked so well for Barbara Melegari at Barilla. By the time her stint is over in Melfi, she will have helped catalyze a new culture of collaborative, self-directed, and inclusive teams.

ADVOCATING AND EMPOWERING

As teams become the engines of organizational change, innovation, and getting things done, they risk being overtaxed. Increasingly empowered teams are an invigorating new direction for organizations, but most organizations need to do a better job in supporting their teams in doing this transformative work.

For all their flexibility, remote and hybrid work models carry their own costs, including the tug-of-war between management and employees on going back to the office. The continual churn of change in the workplace, society, politics, and the environment has contributed to a crisis in the workforce's mental health and well-being.

In this type of environment, it's very difficult for teams to advocate for themselves effectively. They don't have organizational authority and often don't have access to the decision makers and process owners who hold budgets, resources, and systems.

Team leaders must therefore be ready to advocate for their teams. This requires them to tune in to their team's needs, such as access to the resources they need, support in navigating buggy systems, and acknowledgment for their accomplishments.

Being an advocate takes courage because many upper management leaders often don't want to be bothered with what teams need. For those seeking to lead inclusively, they must make it a priority to pick up the phone or walk into a corner office and make the case on their team's behalf. This requires a great deal of conviction and self-motivation. And this is what it takes for teams to break through.

Team leaders must create the conditions their team needs to thrive, whether through advocacy on their behalf or working directly on acquiring the resources needed to achieve their goals. At the same time, they must empower the team to establish their own self-directed ways of working that best fit their goals and their operational constraints.

This dual approach of advocacy and empowerment, combined with practical strategies for leadership development and coordination, is essential for unlocking the collective power of inclusive teams.

ALIGNING THROUGH STORYTELLING

To imagine never-seen-before solutions to never-seen-before problems requires never-heard-before stories. Stories with the potential for catalyzing every team member to action.

Leadership and storytelling are deeply intertwined, tracing back to early human history when tribal leaders used narratives to convey values, share knowledge, and unite communities. One of the major roles of inclusive leaders is to tell the story of the way forward and to inspire teams to be part of that story.

Common purpose—driven by a vision and values—is the storytelling glue that keeps an entire organization focused on how they will work and succeed together. It allows teams to focus on how to best use their collective and individual time, energy, and budgets. It enables them to make tough decisions on how best to respond, or not, to the latest conflagration.

For corporations, there is one well-established common purpose: profit. But then what? How will their products and services improve humanity's lot and make life easier, more equitable, healthier, and safer? How will their working environment nurture people to do their best work? How can an organization enhance the well-being of the community it operates in?

Effective storytelling not only creates a shared vision but also bridges past and present—where we are as an organization and where we want to be—and conveys complex ideas and values that resonate with each team member. It crafts a vivid and inclusive narrative of the future that aligns teams with the overarching goals and genuinely inspires them to make this future a reality.

And it's scalable. Inclusive leaders present powerful "North Star" narratives meant to galvanize and focus every single team in the

P&G'S SWIFFER DUSTS OFF A SELF-DIRECTED TEAM

In the late 1990s, Procter & Gamble (P&G) aimed to innovate within the home cleaning market, which had seen little in the way of groundbreaking products for decades.

The invention was conceived when the director of corporate new ventures was watching his spouse clean and thought, "There has got to be a better way to clean the floor."

But what could that way be?

Coming up with the answer was tasked to a small, multidisciplinary team composed of product designers, engineers, marketers, and consumer researchers whose levels ranged from intern to senior leader.

For the project, initially named "Project Swiffer," this team was empowered to conduct in-depth ethnographic consumer research, prototype various product designs, and test their ideas in real-world settings. The team operated with a high degree of independence, allowing for a rapid iteration of product concepts and designs. This autonomy was crucial for fostering creative problem solving and innovative thinking.

The leaders within P&G allowed the team significant freedom for experimentation and learning from failures, yet they also provided clear objectives and were unequivocal about the team's account-abilities, including demonstrating exceptional collaboration. This collaboration was seen not only within the internal P&G team but also globally when the organization's leaders listened to the team's urging that they license certain technologies from the Japanese company Unicharm, which was not the usual preferred approach. This breakthrough only occurred because the leaders and the team could have an "awkward and honest conversation."

The inclusive leaders at P&G facilitated the success of the team with empathetic coaching that built trust and collaboration so that they could work effectively and independently. They also ensured the team had access to the resources it needed and provided strategic oversight to keep the project aligned with P&G's broader goals. That's what it took to crack the code.

P&G'S SWIFFER DUSTS OFF
A SELF-DIRECTED TEAM

(continued)

The Swiffer—a new type of cleaning product that used disposable cloths to trap and lock in dust and dirt, rather than just moving it around like a traditional mop or dust cloth—was launched in 1999. And it was an instant hit.

It became one of P&G's most successful product launches, spawning an entirely new category in household cleaning, and since then has brought in over $1 billion a year.[2]

---

organization on one overarching goal while leaving it up to each team to determine how they are going to contribute.

Here are a few examples of purpose-driven storylines:

- *Amazon*: "To build a place where people can come to find and discover anything they might want to buy online."
- *Etsy*: "Keep commerce human."
- *Kickstarter*: "To help bring creative projects to life."
- *LinkedIn*: "To connect the world's professionals to make them more productive and successful."
- *Nike*: "To bring inspiration and innovation to every athlete* in the world." (*If you have a body, you are an athlete.)
- *Patagonia*: "We're in business to save our home planet."
- *Warby Parker*: "To offer designer eyewear at a revolutionary price, while leading the way for socially conscious businesses."

Jobs for the Future's (JFF) mission for the past forty years has been to partner with other organizations to build the workforce of today and the future. They do this by designing solutions, scaling best practices, influencing policy and action, and investing in innovation to create learner and worker opportunities as well as strengthen education and career navigation.

Through their new CEO, Maria Flynn, and their board,[3] they set out to update their vision of economic advancement for all to make it tangible and actionable. After a two-year organization-wide, teams-driven process they came up with the following:

"In 10 years, 75 million people in the US facing systemic barriers to advancement will work in quality jobs."

In this narrative "quality jobs" are well-paying jobs with benefits, and with opportunity to grow. This one simple storyline has fully focused and unlocked the collective power of the entire JFF ecosystem, composed of a few hundred partners in corporate, government, education, and nonprofits, to drive this ambitious transformational change.

Howard Schultz, former CEO of Starbucks, offers a compelling example. Schultz often shared his story of growing up in a poor Brooklyn neighborhood, where he experienced the struggles of poverty and the significance of community support.[4] This background deeply shaped Schultz's vision for Starbucks. He aimed to create a "third place," a term coined by sociologist Ray Oldenburg in 1989 designating a space between home and work where people could gather, relax, and connect.[5] Starbucks was not just about selling coffee but about fostering a sense of community and belonging that met the needs of the various locales in which it operated.

By sharing his personal narrative, Schultz emphasized to his leadership team the importance of empathy, respect, and human connection, values that became central to Starbucks' corporate culture. This approach inspired and motivated his leadership team and by extension all employees, encouraging them to see their roles as contributing to a larger purpose than sales and profit. Ultimately, his focus on creating a community-centric atmosphere resonated with his team—Starbucks employees and customers—thus building strong brand loyalty and a supportive work environment.

PULLING IT ALL TOGETHER

For all the focus we have given inclusive teams throughout the book, we still need organizational and team leaders to sponsor and unlock their collective power.

This requires leaders to embrace a more dynamic and inclusive leadership style suited to the evolving demands of modern work environments. Leaders who can navigate these changes effectively are better positioned to facilitate team success and organizational innovation.

Teams are becoming more self-directed and technology-enabled, but inclusive leaders skilled in the areas of human insight, empathy, and strategic oversight will always be needed. Coaching, advocating, empowering, and aligning will ensure leaders' continued relevance in modern organizations.

CHAPTER 9 SUMMARY

- Self-directed teams require facilitative leaders who can adapt to and shape the conditions for their teams to collectively do their best work.

- Trust and collaboration can be achieved through coaching with empathy and encouraging empathetic peer coaching. When team members feel heard and valued, their accountability to the team and its goals increases.

- Empowered teams need leaders who advocate for them—who exhibit the courage to confront adversity and voice the team's needs.

- It takes more than just goal-setting to align a team; creating an inspirational narrative of the future focuses every team in the organization on one overarching goal while leaving it up to each team to determine how they are going to contribute.

10

A New Direction for DE&I

Do not be satisfied with the stories that come before you.
Unfold your own myth.

—Rumi, thirteenth-century Persian
poet and Sufi mystic

THE WAY WE SEE IT, the Racial Reckoning of 2020 that became the DE&I Backlash of 2023 is set to become the Breakthrough Reinvention of the next decade.

Let us explain.

Back in 2020, after George Floyd's murder, many champions of diversity couldn't help themselves from saying, "Seems like this time it will be different." It *did* feel different. CEOs were making denunciations against "systemic racism" and were wading into tackling "equity."

A critical mass of powers-that-be, from corporate executives to politicians to community leaders and even chiefs of police, were chastened enough to admit they actually weren't doing so well on "this diversity thing" and those "random pockets of discrimination" weren't so random after all. Their naïve views were blown to smithereens in the wake of an unarmed Black man being asphyxiated for eight minutes, twenty seconds on video until his last words, "I can't breathe," presaged his death.

Energy, time, and millions of dollars poured into anti-racism, anti-discrimination, and inclusion efforts followed the exhortations and outrage. Town halls with "courageous conversations" popped up every-where. Chief diversity officer (CDO) roles proliferated in companies of all sizes in all industries. Diversity budgets got a pop and many DE&I leadership roles were created where there hadn't been any.

So many promises were made. And they all sounded good and sincere and game-changing.

Then came the raging counterforces of backlash. Corporations were attacked by name for their "woke" commitments to DE&I. Some compa-nies backed off because the bad publicity wasn't worth it and the voices of the skeptical and resistant within their walls were growing louder.

And so, a good number of DE&I budgets tightened up and implemen-tations were delayed.

In 2022 the attrition rate in DE&I roles in US companies was 33 percent, versus 21 percent for non-DE&I roles at S&P 500 companies,[1] with the average tenure of chief diversity officers being less than two years—one of the shortest among all executive roles. Many who did not lose their jobs or abandon them saw their DE&I roles downgraded.

For at least a decade before the DE&I backlash began, the signs have been there that DE&I was not evolving to keep up with the changing times. Korn Ferry's study on DE&I post-2020, "Real Progress or Just For Show?,"[2] raised serious concerns about the maturity of many organizations' DE&I efforts. Over five thousand business leaders told us it was still too focused on events, feel-good messaging, and the right thing to do. These, of course, are fundamental worthwhile objectives, but they are only first steps and we should be further along.

"We can't cheerlead our way to a DE&I transformation," says Korn Ferry Senior Partner Cathi Rittelmann, who also serves as Leadership Accelerators Solution Lead. "Leaders keep asking, as we've all asked at some point on a long trip, 'Are we there yet?' They want to move on to the next phase because they think their organizations are 'there.' But they are far from that—because it's not a check-a-box exercise but rather a full overhaul journey."

All along DE&I should have been expanding its relevance—and therefore justification for budgets and resources—by providing compelling evidence that DE&I efforts are key enablers to core business objectives.

In fact, we have been tackling this challenge from different angles throughout the Five Inclusive Disciplines trilogy.

- **In book one on Inclusive Leadership**: Given the massive disruption our societies are undergoing, inclusive leaders are needed to navigate teams and organizations though rapid change and increasing polarization. We need leaders that can inspire and enable all kinds of talent to rise to their full potential. We need leaders who can facilitate diverse teams in what they can do best: cultivate innovation and drive business results.

- **In book two on Inclusive Organizations**: We showed how DE&I is a vital enabler to the key organizational objectives, namely managing risks and enhancing corporate performance and reputation. Inclusive organizations do this by ensuring the systemic levers of the organization—policies, processes, procedures, structures—are inclusive, equitable, and sustainable. They root out elements that inadvertently favor certain groups over others and design systems that allow equal access, opportunity, and visibility so that the best talent, ideas, and initiatives can rise to the top.

- **In this book three on Inclusive Teams**: We have been making the case that teams, as the smallest unit of an organization's culture, represent the level at which meaningful change is both accessible and scalable. The individualistic concept that inclusive leaders elevate individual talent is limiting. Team leaders *and* team members must empower, enable, and hold themselves accountable to act in ways that unlock their collective power and achieve innovative and breakthrough results throughout the organization.

The reckoning is here.

Al mal viento, buena cara, as the Latin American saying goes. *To a harsh wind, a strong face.*

This reinvention of how DE&I looks, feels, and drives results is how we make it indispensable to the organizations.

FROM RECKONING TO REINVENTION

Historically, the DE&I office has taken a top-down, bottom-up approach: working with senior leaders at the top to cascade initiatives down, and with employee resource groups to reach the wide base of employees at the lower levels.

The new layered-in approach must include a focus on teams. This is how we ensure diversity, equity, and inclusion is viscerally experienced— not just as slogans or groups advocating for their own needs—but as the psychological safety necessary to do one's best work individually and collaboratively.

Here's how:

- Be Strategic About Innovation
- Enroll Middle Managers
- Dismantle Outdated Role Qualifications
- Leverage Intersectionality as a Performance Superpower

BE STRATEGIC ABOUT INNOVATION

The promise of DE&I is that greater diversity will lead to greater creativity and innovation, something we explored in chapter 8. But the reality is that DE&I practitioners are rarely focused on fulfilling this worthy goal. And as the last few years have shown, if they don't figure out how to make it a priority, DE&I will sink even deeper into organizational irrelevancy.

The DE&I field has long sought to create disruptive organizations that are more diverse, equitable, and inclusive. Now it's imperative that it take a look in the mirror and disrupt itself. To achieve the activation of inclusive teams throughout the organization it must recast the profile of CDO and redesign DE&I governance.

The CDO role must transform from one of compliance, awareness, social justice, and PR to one grounded in business, that is driven by data, and that is focused on outcomes and commercial impact.

Next-generation CDOs have an extraordinary opportunity to be the catalysts for business transformation, setting the precedent for how inclusive teams can be a powerhouse for innovation and success in any organization. As champions of inclusion, they not only create a space where every voice is heard but also where these voices can synchronize to produce a symphony of innovative ideas. Their strategic initiatives to embed diversity and inclusion into the organizational DNA enables companies to tap into a wider range of market insights and customer needs, translating into products and services that resonate with a broader audience. Moreover, inclusive teams led by culturally adept CDOs are more agile and better equipped to navigate the complexities of global markets. By leveraging the collective intelligence of a diverse workforce, CDOs can drive performance and results that not only meet but exceed expectations.

We have worked with a large number of CDOs, and what we have seen is that many could be stronger in the inclusive leader competencies of cultivating innovation and driving results. This has to change.

Next-generation CDOs are going to have to be strategic, systemic-thinking, data-informed leaders. With their high profile and enterprise-wise remits—and likely smaller budgets and staffs—they're going to have to be masterful at influence and persuasion in managing disparate stakeholders. These competencies not only will help them address enterprise-wide strategies, but also position inclusive teams as the scalable units of innovation they can be.

CDO positions will have to undergo transformational change and so too will the governance structures supporting the work.

Often CDOs have not been well positioned within their organizations—either they're placed too high or too low in relation to the organization's level of DE&I maturity. Regardless of where the CDO reports, the DE&I office should never see itself as a stand-alone function. It must always work as an integrating and collaborative practice whose ultimate goal is to unlock the collective power of the organization to break through.

If diversity's reckoning can lead to this next-generation repositioning, we will be able to look at this crucible as the wake-up call we needed and heeded.

ENROLL MIDDLE MANAGERS

Middle managers are the most critical determinant for whether employees will practice the 5 Disciplines of Inclusive Teams. This massive and influential layer within organizations is often referred to as the "frozen middle"—because this is where DE&I efforts are most likely to stall.

Efforts aimed at melting the resistance in this layer have had minimal effect. We believe that this is due to an ineffective set of tactics on the part of DE&I practitioners. Here's what hasn't worked:

- Complaining that managers are the cause for DE&I dying on the vine in organizations,
- Exhorting managers to step it up without providing them with practical tools and enabling processes, and
- Training on DE&I that leaves out DE&I's supreme relevance to more effective execution and production.

Middle managers' field of play is limited, so the business-case messages that work at the strategic C-suite level mean little to them. These managers don't have their hands on the key levers of enterprise systems nor do they have the authority to mobilize the masses; their main area of influence is driving the accountability of their teams. This is *their* "so what": increased productivity, enhanced safety on a factory floor, accelerated continuous improvement. We need to show them that their "how" is diverse, inclusive, self-directed teams that can unlock their collective power.

This is the hook to enroll middle managers in DE&I: tapping their role-based motivations and providing them with the 5 Disciplines of Inclusive Teams as a means for their teams to achieve them.

Building on the tips that were shared in part 1, here are a couple of strategies organizations can adopt to engage middle managers in, for example, two prominent industry sectors:

- **Retail**: Store managers can design and roll out enhancing-the-shopper-experience workshops whose participants are diverse-by-design teams composed of store staff as well as employees from corporate functions (Marketing, Merchandising, Finance, etc.), two populations that rarely directly interact in person, to problem-solve together for the overlooked shopper. Such workshops should prioritize the exchange of information and ideas between store staff and corporate functions as well as among store staff, with guidance from corporate colleagues on which best practices can be leveraged.
- **Factory**: Managers have long used standard operating procedures (SOPs) and lean manufacturing principles to reduce variability and enhance workflow efficiency. Paradoxically, by taking it a step further and inviting some disruptive thinking in updating the

SOPs, managers can develop open and inclusive feedback processes to further synchronization and ensure that production processes accommodate a diversity of worker needs and abilities—for example, SOPs accessible in multiple formats (different languages, large print, audio, video, braille, and so on).

DISMANTLE OUTDATED ROLE QUALIFICATIONS

Inclusive organizations and leaders are turning away from traditional job qualifications and successfully finding talent in historically overlooked places.

"A big shift is underway in how the labor market recognizes talent," wrote Cat Ward, former vice president at Jobs for the Future, and Aneesh Raman, vice president and workforce expert at LinkedIn, in a 2023 *Forbes* article, with roughly one in four job postings in the United States no longer requiring degrees (24 percent, up from 15 percent in 2020), according to data from LinkedIn.[3]

Rather than a lowering of standards, this is great news for business. Why? As Ward and Raman write, "Traditional signals such as specific years of experience are flawed predictors of someone's ability to do a job well." Furthermore, while over 70 percent of jobs state they require college degrees, less than 50 percent of the US workforce holds a bachelor's degree. Getting rid of outdated job qualifications is an important step to addressing this manufactured labor shortage.

And as David Kenney, executive chairman of Nielsen, explained, "Skills are the future of work—not a one-and-done degree."[4]

Not only is a focus on skills instead of degrees a means to access more talent, but it's also a means to creating more diverse, and therefore stronger and more innovative, teams. This is the way out of the structural conundrum in various key industries like engineering that have long suffered from a homogenous talent pool (often White and Asian males). While strengthening the degreed pipeline of women and other racial minorities may take a generation, dismantling unnecessary degree requirements opens up the pipeline everywhere in one fell swoop.

But, as we have discussed, the true value of hiring people from diverse backgrounds only gets realized when their different perspectives, skill sets, and ideas are leveraged to make new and innovative strategic choices. More than simply eliminating a bias toward certain backgrounds in the hiring process, this bias needs to be eliminated from the organizational culture, which as we know, is most viscerally experienced at the team level. This is where the 5 Disciplines come in; practicing them creates an inclusive team culture that protects and celebrates the individuality of each member for the benefit of the team and its goals.

LEVERAGE INTERSECTIONALITY AS A PERFORMANCE SUPERPOWER

Agi is a young professional and first-generation Mexican American. While she's proud of her heritage, the messages she heard from mainstream society and from her immigrant parents were a *guiso* (stew) of mixed messages of assimilation, be proud of your heritage, go succeed in American mainstream society but hold on to traditional genderized Mexican ways. As a young adult she pursued community counseling and has practiced trauma-centered healing as a licensed therapist for many years. But all along, she has struggled with imposter syndrome (she was in the minority in most of the circles she ran in). This limited her effectiveness; she vacillated between showing up as her assimilated self and owning her authentic immigrant, bicultural Mexican American identity, especially as her practice's clients became significantly more diverse.

In coaching Agi on inclusive leadership, Andrés explored how she could allow the various layers of her identity—Latina, parent, passionate and fierce advocate for those enduring trauma, and so on—to manifest in their full intersectionality.

There was a time when Agi self-identified as Agi Semrad. Then, she made one simple but defining decision that led to her breaking out of her assimilated self and into her more multidimensional intersectional self: Agi reclaimed her last name, Corona, which she had forfeited when she got married. When she took that step of reflecting her Latina self in Corona and her intercultural self in keeping her husband's name, Semrad, she affirmed her heritage and her intersectional intercultural identity. This reclaiming and renaming marked a shift in how her team sees and listens to her. Some did not even know of her Latina heritage; now they had a clear line to how that aspect of her identity influences some of her mission-oriented priorities. Now, in her practice, Agi and her team engage with their clients from often overlooked groups more authentically, helping them reclaim the fullness of their intersectional identities.

Intersectionality is a powerful and authentic way to address the reality of every single person's multidimensional diversity, including that of the dominant group in the Global North (White, Christian, heterosexual males). The traditional approach by DE&I has been to create awareness of this reality—everyone has an intersectional identity! DE&I now needs to evolve its exploration of intersectionality so that teams can reap its benefits. The next step for DE&I practitioners is to support team members in the necessary discovery process of their own intersectional identities and develop the Cultural Dexterity to tap into those differences—within themselves and others. The result? Better decisions and more effective collaboration that translate to higher performance and positive transformation.

PULLING IT ALL TOGETHER

ERGs, diversity councils, and DE&I training, while all important *enablers*, are not the *outcomes* that DE&I should be seeking. Join us in this new direction for DE&I to gain the means to producing inclusive teams and greater innovation, better customer service, growth in new markets, and more optimized talent.

Let the reactionary forces argue against this!

CHAPTER 10 SUMMARY

- A shift in how DE&I looks, feels, and drives business results is how we make it indispensable to organizations.

- The role of middle managers is increasing productivity and accelerating continuous improvement. Show them that their *how* is diverse, inclusive, self-directed teams that can unlock their collective power.

- The CDO role must transform from one of compliance, awareness, social justice, and PR to one that is grounded in business, driven by data, and focused on outcomes and commercial impact.

- Not only is a focus on skills instead of outdated qualifications like degrees a means to access more talent, but it is also a means to creating more diverse, and therefore stronger and more innovative, teams.

- Diversity must consistently be understood through an intersectional lens—otherwise a team's inclusiveness will remain superficial.

CONCLUSION

The Unbreakable Thread of Human Connection

TEAMS ARE WHERE IT'S AT. In a world of never-ending, high-velocity disruption, teams are the most agile units within organizations. That means they are, simultaneously, the catalysts for continual innovation as well as for organizational transformation. This is why CEOs are urgently seeking to move decision-making down to the middle of the organization, where the majority of teams reside. Fortunately, technological advances now make this more feasible than ever.

To be transformative, teams must celebrate and protect the individuality of each team member while creating a unity of purpose. In other words, they need to both celebrate their differences and channel them toward a shared purpose. This is the challenge and the source of breakthrough potential for teams.

In part 1, we explored how teams can address this challenge and unlock their collective power through the 5 Disciplines: Connecting, Caring, Synchronizing, Cultural Dexterity, and Powersharing. The disciplines are foundational capabilities and habits crucial for leveraging the diversity within teams to achieve breakthrough performance and success. We introduced several key practices grounded in research that teams can adopt to embody each of the disciplines.

In part 2 we looked at the exciting implications of inclusive teams for innovation, leadership, and the practice of diversity, equity, and inclusion within organizations. In the appendix, we leave you with a Coaching Guide for Inclusive Teams that will walk team leaders and members through a turnkey journey to develop and apply the 5 Disciplines.

What have we left unsaid?

At the speed of change we are experiencing, plenty. These are the last things we want to call out.

Tactically and strategically, we will need to measure the impact of teams in new ways. Teams should consider defining key performance indicators (KPIs) that include both *lagging* indicators of team performance, such as financial indices and stakeholders' satisfaction metrics, as well as *leading* indicators, typically operational metrics such as quality, timeliness, compliance, and efficiency.

Humility-wise, we need to get comfortable with uncertainty. Nowadays, so much more of what we are all doing is experimental. We must be in continual iterative solution-making mode, moving with confidence when we are onto something with our teams, while at the same time not being dogmatic and rigid about any one way forward.

Courage-wise, we must be willing to take on more risks while holding ourselves and our teams accountable for daily responsibilities and deliverables.

People-wise, we must not allow screens, AI, and virtual spaces to come between us and the humanity of our team members. This is one we want to emphatically highlight. For all the advancements we've made, for all the efficiency and productivity we've gained, for all the new concepts introduced here, at the heart of it all are people—our team members, each with a story that's as unique as it's universal.

It's our humanity that makes us truly innovative, resilient, and inclusive. Our ability to connect with, care for, and celebrate each other in all our diversity is what drives us forward.

Together. Whenever and wherever. In our Inclusive Teams.

■   ■   ■

Charting a Path to an Inclusive Team

A Guide for Team Members and Team Leaders

THE STEPS HERE CAN BE FACILITATED by a team leader along with the rest of the team or they can be supplemented with the expertise of a consultant who can provide a third-party perspective along with specialized expertise.

There are four phases to getting a team on the pathway to becoming an inclusive team.

- Phase 1: Team purpose and formation
- Phase 2: Team engagement and assessment
- Phase 3: Team alignment
- Phase 4: Team development acceleration

PHASE 1: TEAM PURPOSE AND FORMATION

1. Make the Clear Case for Being an Inclusive Team

Before engaging in a formal process for team development work, the team leader and the team members should align on the scope, timeline, and detailed activities of the work and be clear about each team member's role and responsibilities. The case for the work must be clearly laid out in unambiguous terms. For example:

> "The team is engaging in a process to ensure its full potential is unlocked. To achieve this, the team will apply the 5 Disciplines of Inclusive Teams to how it defines its work, how it structures its processes, and how members behave toward one another."

2. Define Key Stakeholders

Next, identify the different parties who have a stake in the team's work and purpose.

Who is on the team? This may seem obvious, but teams often have fuzzy boundaries, their exact composition varying depending on whom you ask. Are all members direct reports of the team leader? Is there a core team and an extended team?

Who else needs to participate or be informed about the team's work? Every organization is different, but common stakeholders may include the board (in the case of a C-suite team), PE partners (in the case of a PE-backed C-suite), or internal DE&I or HR practitioners.

PHASE 2: TEAM ENGAGEMENT AND ASSESSMENT

The focus here is to ensure all key stakeholders are engaged in an open and positive way to ensure their strong buy-in and high-quality contributions from the onset of the journey.

This can be achieved by having clear and comprehensive communications, whether virtual or in person, about the purpose and "mechanics" of the development journey. Holding a live kickoff call or in-person meeting with all team members can be effective in presenting the rationale for the work, sharing existing research behind the approach, and offering a detailed view of the journey and expectations from all participants to help ensure positive outcomes.

Once objectives have been shared with the team, the following workstreams can occur.

1. Collectively Shape an Inclusive Team Vision

When and where possible, it's always best to have an offsite kickoff. To prepare for this, the team leader works with the team to shape a clear and compelling vision for building an inclusive team, elaborating on the early discussions that led to starting the development journey work. This can be done through structured interviews with the team leader, complemented by the members' independent reflections and writing. During the process, team leaders should address the following questions:

- What will having a more inclusive team contribute to the team's purpose and goals?
- Looking at the team's work, where will each of the 5 Disciplines have the greatest potential for positive impact?
- What structural and behavioral aspects of the team's work offer the greatest opportunities for applying the 5 Disciplines?

To shape their point of view on these questions, the team leader can solicit the help of their chief of staff, their HR and DE&I partners, and/or their consultant. The final output, which may be a couple of pages long, will be key for preparing for the team alignment and future leadership communications work.

2. Gather Insights About Strengths and Gaps

Team leaders (and the consultant if one is involved) should work with team members to align on what the team's strengths and development opportunities are. To achieve this work, practitioners may use a combination of online survey and interviews to assess 1) the extent to which the team currently exhibits each of the 5 Disciplines of Inclusive Teams, 2) where they perceive the greater opportunities for development, and 3) what ideas could be considered to close capability gaps. Here are some sample questions to consider:

- How do team members *connect* formally and informally?
- How does the team leader encourage team members to *care* about each other?
- What work processes enable team members to *synchronize* their work?
- How has the team benefited from the *cultural dexterity* of one or several of its members?

- How can team members *powershare* across the purpose and projects within the team?

PHASE 3: TEAM ALIGNMENT

The team's work centers on building a shared understanding of development priorities and outlining a strategy to accelerate the team's progression toward operating as an inclusive team.

The team leader and team members next design the agenda and contents of the team's alignment offsite (usually one or two days in duration). Although there are no two identical designs, effective offsites typically include any combination of the following modules.

1. **Define the Team's Work**

    The team leader plays a critical role in providing a guiding vision for what being an inclusive team means and how it links to the organization's purpose and strategic objectives. Team leaders must strike the right balance between setting clear boundaries and keeping a safe and open space for development and innovative thinking. Among the different topics the team leader may include in their opening framing statement:

    - Sharing their personal experience with inclusive teams,
    - Linking inclusive team and organizational vision, culture, and performance,
    - Proposing norms that align with the 5 Disciplines,
    - Clarifying expectations from stakeholders.

2. **Build Consensus on Team Development Priorities**

    Providing feedback to the team on their collective inputs from phase 1 is a critical feature of the team alignment. When preparing this segment of the offsite, discussions in pairs and small groups, facilitated by consultants, can help uncover questions and foster greater engagement, dialogue, and ownership.

3. **Learn Best Practices**

    Tapping the team's pool of knowledge and experiences is powerful. Often, the team's questions can be best answered by the team itself by mining each member's resources. For example, one member may share when in their career they have felt most connected to their team or what it was about the way that team was set up and did its work that made them feel connected. These experiences can then be codified into best practices. Team members can powershare by taking turns in leading these discussions. To complement this learning-from-within, the team facilitator can supplement the work of the team by sharing best practices of highly inclusive leaders and teams (e.g., rotational meeting leadership, team activities outside the office, immersive learning events).

4. **Define Fit-For-Purpose Ways of Working**

There are typically two main avenues to drive change. One relates to the *structural* changes that can enable a team to do its work in more inclusive ways. The other concerns the *behavioral* changes that team members can make to realize their aspirations for greater inclusion.

In both cases, a shift in *mindset* needs to occur on the part of all team members that will support the design and implementation of both structural and behavioral changes.

PHASE 4: TEAM DEVELOPMENT ACCELERATION

There are various strategies teams can pursue to accelerate their transformational development. What these strategies have in common is a need to pause to develop more self-awareness, the foundational starting point of any kind of sustainable and effective change. Here are a couple of ways to do this:

1. **Enhance Self-Awareness**

At the Individual Level

- *Reflective Practices.* Encourage team members to journal, meditate, or do mindful breathing exercises. These practices help individuals become more aware of their thoughts, feelings, and behaviors, contributing to greater self-awareness.

- *Constructive Feedback Mechanisms.* Structured and safe feedback mechanisms through regular one-on-one meetings, peer reviews, or feedback sessions that are framed positively and constructively can unlock enhanced team performance.

- *Professional Development.* Offer opportunities for professional development that include workshops or training sessions focused on emotional intelligence, communication skills, and other areas that contribute to self-awareness.

At the Team Level

- *Team Reflection Sessions.* Schedule regular team reflection sessions where members can share their views, experiences, and feelings about ongoing projects and team dynamics. These sessions can be short (twenty minutes), embedded in the team's *flow of work*, or scheduled as stand-alone sessions during a team offsite.

- *Group Mindfulness Practices.* Guided team meditations or mindfulness-based stress-reduction programs can enhance collective focus, empathy, and awareness.

- *Cultivating a Culture of Openness.* Encourage team members to share their successes and failures, learning experiences, and personal growth stories without fear of judgment. Practitioners at Korn Ferry often use the WeConnect framework of Dimensions of Diversity to help teams engage on this type of development work.

2. **Track Progress**

   As teams set a timeline for change, they will need to determine when an appropriate time is to take stock of progress and consider what actions may still be needed to close gaps or rectify the team's course. Teams may launch another round of surveys and feedback loops using the same tools as in phase 2. When conducting this follow-up assessment, it is important to apply the same standards of confidentiality, anonymity, and focus on the actionable insights described earlier.

ADDITIONAL CONSIDERATIONS

Throughout the four phases described previously, teams may consider a few more design options that will help the team achieve greater progress toward greater inclusion.

PRACTICE, PRACTICE, PRACTICE

Years of working as team development consultants have shown us that practice does not always make perfect, but it certainly makes for improvement. Having a team apply their specific work processes or team norms to solving a real-world business question (for example, what policy should we apply regarding remote work?), and being observed and coached by a team development practitioner while doing so, can often be a great feature for a team development offsite.

PLAN, PLAN, PLAN

Sustained change requires planning and support. As the team defines a list of changes to make it more inclusive, it will need a clear plan of action and clear accountabilities for executing the plan. Internal or external practitioners can help the team by offering a template they will complete and that will list the following items:

- List and timeline of changes that will happen and when (for example, redesign of team meetings, change in governance, creation of new team norms, etc.),
- Resources needed to implement changes successfully (for example, individual and team coaching, learning sessions, consultation with internal or external resources, etc.),
- Accountabilities of individuals and the team for executing the plan, and
- Communicating to stakeholders regarding the plan (for example, who needs to be engaged in the process and in what role?).

TIPS FOR STAKEHOLDERS

Finally, here are a few tips for all stakeholders likely to take part in the team development journey.

Tips for stakeholders to optimize inclusive team dynamics

TEAM LEADER	TEAM MEMBERS	INTERNAL OR EXTERNAL PRACTITIONERS
• *Embrace collective team leadership.* Resist the urge to "figure it all out" for the team and instead focus on the big picture and empower the team to solve for greater team inclusion.	• *Combine curiosity with a challenging mindset.* Engage in the process with courageous questions for yourself and others. Offer equal parts questions and solutions.	• *Manage boundaries.* Your power for influence depends on your ability to remain an objective, unbiased party in this process. Avoid saying "we" when referring to the team and set time for the team to be together without you present.
• *Coach the team.* Lead by example to encourage collaboration, discovery, and divergent thinking in pursuit of positive change.	• *Retain a dynamic view of the team.* Learn to recognize and share with others where you see hidden potential for the team and team members to be more inclusive and ways for the team to progress.	• *Team up.* This is a team sport. You will offer greater value to the team by teaming with other practitioners who can broaden your perspective and challenge your biases.

APPENDIX B

Previous Research and Korn Ferry Research
The Science of Inclusive Teams

W HAT IS THE SECRET SAUCE OF DIVERSE teams acting inclusively that generates better results? We have been among the
scientists and practitioners who have attempted to find out.

Researchers and relationship experts Brené Brown and Amy Edmondson have been deeply influential in laying down the relational and
psychological fundamentals of what makes teams attractive, strong, and
productive.

Brené Brown's focus has been on the work we as individuals can do to
fortify our own sense of self-love and, from that, more meaningfully
connect with and love others in their personal lives and on the work team.
But this is not soft stuff. This is the foundation for increased power in our
personal and work lives, she argues. The key to this is to confront the
stigma of shame (as recipients and perpetrators). Brown breaks this down
into a seven-step process and notes that to address shame we must
increase our trust of others while at the same time more confidently
instilling trust on the part of others in us.

Amy Edmondson's breakthrough work has been on the role of *psychological safety* in teams. She sees it as the key condition for being able to
take interpersonal risks and breaks down what it takes for individuals in a

team to nurture this type of environment. Curiosity, passion, and empathy, she proves, are the ingredients that then foster safer spaces to bring forth new ideas that deepen the collaborations that effective teams require.

Brown starts with the inner work individuals must do before they confidently and effectively engage those around them, including their teams. Edmondson does the reverse; she starts with the work teams must do to create the conditions that then allow individuals to act with more confidence and effectiveness. Both approaches are right and true in their reciprocity.

On the current borders of their work is our research on the diversity of teams. We explore on a deeper level what it takes for heterogenous groups of people to feel included and how people's identities impact team dynamics and performance.

TEAM CHEMISTRY IS NOT JUST A METAPHOR

There is another field of relevant research that we must also bring into this exploration. Dr. Anita Woolley and her colleagues are early pioneers in exploring the neuropsychological dimensions of teams. Their work has focused on what they refer to as *collective intelligence*, which is a group's ability to perform cognitive tasks, such as problem solving or decision-making, more effectively than the sum of its individual members' abilities. She posits that collective intelligence is enhanced when team members have a diversity of perspectives and backgrounds as well as inclusive mindset and attitudes.

Dr. Woolley's research has shown that teams that are over 60 percent female but not more than 70 percent female perform better at achieving team outcomes than teams with no or little gender diversity. A study by Korn Ferry in collaboration with Dr. Woolley and the MSCI (a Wall Street-based provider of critical decision support tools and services for the global investment community) demonstrated that teams led by inclusive leaders (as measured by Korn Ferry's validated psychometrical assessment of inclusive leaders) also perform more effectively.

Dr. Hannah Critchlow's 2022 book *Joined-Up Thinking* is a narrative compendium on how collective intelligence is fueled by our brain's neurotransmitters (among them serotonin, oxytocin, dopamine, and endorphins). In it, Dr. Critchlow has more than one hundred pages of citations proving two powerful concepts: First, that our personal performance and decision-making is enhanced when the four different lobes of our brains (the parietal, occipital, temporal, and frontal) and the various sensory cortexes (among them, auditory, visual, sensory) are collaborating with each other. Second, this synergistic phenomenon *within* an individual brain replicates and scales when a collection of brains engage each other in the context of a team.

This is what Critchlow calls "joined-up thinking." When this happens, it exponentially improves a team's ability to engage in divergent thinking and, with that, be more innovative and have a greater impact on its outcomes. As Steven Sloman and Philip Fernbach summarized in their book *The Knowledge Illusion: Why We Never Think Alone*, "Individuals rely not only on knowledge stored within our skulls but also on knowledge stored elsewhere: in our bodies, in the environment, and especially in other people."[5]

As we see it, these are neurological explanations for out-of-the-box thinking. If we overemphasize thinking within the "box" of the frontal lobe, we get trapped in our cognitive perceptions of the world around us. Conversely, if we over rely on the temporal lobe "box," we limit ourselves to thoughts and actions that cater to our emotions. Out-of-the-box thinking, therefore, is when we more deliberately and expertly draw from our individual as well as collective brain's multiple modalities of perceiving, sensing, interpreting, and acting.

But how can we do this more "deliberately and expertly"? This is what we set out to find out and shared in this book.

■　　■　　■

The Five Inclusive Disciplines Trilogy Models

The Inclusive Leader, Inclusive Teams, and Inclusive Organizations

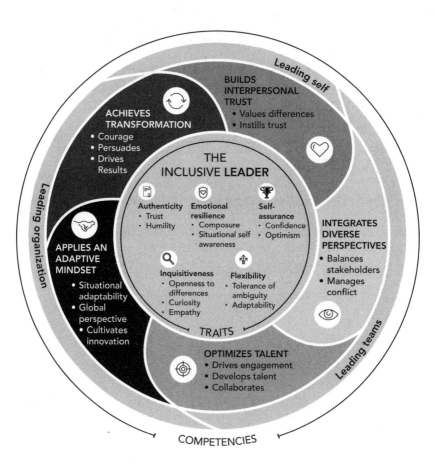

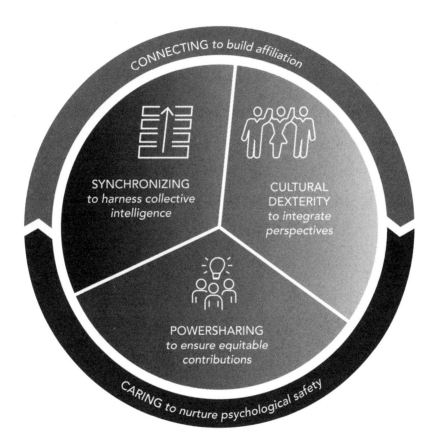

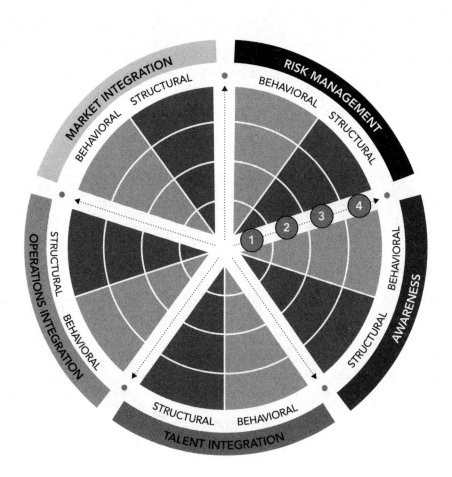

NOTES

Introduction

1. Dan Milmo and agency, "ChatGPT Reaches 100 Million Users Two Months After Launch," *The Guardian*, February 2, 2023, https://www.theguardian.com/technology/2023/feb/02/chatgpt-100-million-users-open-ai-fastest-growing-app.

2. "The State of Business Communications 2023," Grammarly & The Harris Poll, https://go.grammarly.com/l/894581/2023-02-10/4nh62.

3. "Enterprise Agility in Financial Services: The New Strategic Imperative," Accenture, 2018, https://www.accenture.com/content/dam/accenture/final/a-com-migration/manual/pdf/careers/pdf-43/Accenture-Enterprise-Agility-Web.pdf.

4. "Achieving Greater Agility: The Essential Influence of the C-Suite," PMI Thought Leadership Series, https://i.forbesimg.com/forbesinsights/pmi/achieving_greater_agility.pdf.

5. Kate Vitasek, "Why Collaboration Yields Improved Productivity (And The Science Behind It)," *Forbes*, March 8, 2022, https://www.forbes.com/sites/katevitasek/2022/03/08/why-collaboration-yields-improved-productivity-and-the-science-behind-it/?sh=29dc19485d55.

6. "How Soft Skills Are Crucial to Your Business," Salesforce, August 20, 2014, https://www.salesforce.com/ca/blog/how-soft-skills-are-crucial-to-your-business.

7. Interview by Andrés Tapia, April 2023.

8. Conversation with Yum! EIB Team by Andrés Tapia, November 12, 2023.

9. Bruce Crumley, "Bayer's American CEO Plots Management Revolution from Above," *Inc*, March 22, 2024, https://www.inc.com/bruce-crumley/bayers-american-ceo-plots-management-revolution-from-above.html.

10. Bill Anderson, "Bayer CEO: Corporate Bureaucracy Belongs in the 19th Century. Here's How We're Fighting It," *Fortune*, March 21, 2024, https://fortune-com.cdn.ampproject.org/c/s/fortune.com/2024/03/21/bayer-ceo-bill-anderson-corporate-bureaucracy-19th-century-leadership/amp.

11. Sid Probstein, "Reality Check: Still Spending More Time Gathering Instead of Analyzing," *Forbes*, December 17, 2019, https://www.forbes.com/sites/forbestechcouncil/2019/12/17/reality-check-still-spending-more-time-gathering-instead-of-analyzing/?sh=133a2d5d28ff.

12. Priyanka B. Carr and Gregory M. Walton, "Cues of Working Together Fuel Intrinsic Motivation," *Journal of Experimental Social Psychology* 53 (July 2014): 169–184, https://www.sciencedirect.com/science/article/abs/pii/S0022103114000420?via=ihub.

13. Anderson, "Bayer CEO."

14. "Nearly 80% of Companies Worldwide Rank Innovation as a Top-Three Priority for 2023," *BCG*, May 23, 2023, https://www.bcg.com/press/23may2023-companies-rank-innovation-as-top-three-priority-2023.

15. "Hacking Diversity With Inclusive Decision-Marking," *CloverPop*, https://www.cloverpop.com/hubfs/Whitepapers/Cloverpop_Hacking_Diversity_Inclusive_Decision_Making_White_Paper.pdf.

16. David Rock, Heidi Grant, and Jacqui Grey, "Diverse Teams Feel Less Comfortable—and That's Why They Perform Better," *Harvard Business Review*, September 22, 2016, https://hbr .org/2016/09/diverse-teams-feel-less-comfortable-and-thats-why-they-perform-better.

17. Stuart R. Levine, "Diversity Confirmed To Boost Innovation And Financial Results," *Forbes*, January 15, 2020, https://www.forbes.com/sites/forbesinsights/2020/01/15/diversity -confirmed-to-boost-innovation-and-financial-results/?sh=50c8c785c4a6.

18. Interview by Amelia Haynes, February 15, 2024.

19. Amelia Haynes and Michael Platt, "Mind to Mind," Korn Ferry, https://www.kornferry.com /content/dam/kornferry-v2/pdf/institute/kfi-mind-to-mind.pdf.

Chapter 1

1. "The Loneliness Epidemic Persists: A Post-Pandemic Look at the State of Loneliness among U.S. Adults," The Cigna Group, https://newsroom.thecignagroup.com/loneliness-epidemic -persists-post-pandemic-look.

2. "The Loneliness Epidemic Persists."

3. Adam Wood, "Meet the Future-Minded Leader: Your Organizations' Answer to Uncertainty," *BetterUp* (blog), January 11, 2022, https://www.betterup.com/blog/insights-report-future -minded-leader?hs_preview=wtBSbiQA-62370069174.

4. Michael Dickerson, "Loneliness in the Age of Flexible Work: Statistics and Solutions," LinkedIn, July 13, 2022, https://www.linkedin.com/pulse/loneliness-age-flexible-work -statistics-solutions-michael-dickerson#:~:text=The%20research%20speaks%20for%20itself .&text=72%25%20percent%20of%20employees%20report,at%20least%20once%20a%20 month.

5. Alain Hunkins, "Three Innovative Solutions for Overcoming Workplace Loneliness," *Forbes*, March 15, 2023, https://www.forbes.com/sites/alainhunkins/2023/03/15/three-innovative -solutions-for-overcoming-workplace-loneliness/?sh=326790bd1450.

6. Adam Smiley Poswolsky, "How Leaders Can Build Connection in a Disconnected Workplace," *Harvard Business Review*, January 21, 2022, https://hbr.org/2022/01/how-leaders-can-build -connection-in-a-disconnected-workplace#:~:text=Employee%20disconnection%20is%20 one%20of,and%20lower%20quality%20of%20work.

7. Naz Baheshti, "10 Timely Statistics About the Connection Between Employee Engagement and Wellness," *Forbes*, January 16, 2019, https://www.forbes.com/sites/nazbeheshti/2019/01 /16/10-timely-statistics-about-the-connection-between-employee-engagement-and-wellness /?sh=3e37288a22a0.

8. Maggie Wooll, MBA, "Your Workforce Is Lonely. It's Hurting Your Business," *BetterUp* (blog), June 14, 2022, https://www.betterup.com/blog/connection-crisis-impact-on-work.

9. "The State of Workplace Connection Report: Examining the Role of Connection in Driving Employee Happiness and Retention," Blueboard, https://fs.hubspotusercontent00.net/hubfs /6173605/Original%20Research%20Report/Blueboard_StateOfWorkplaceConnection-2022 .pdf.

10. Jim Harter, "Employee Engagement vs. Employee Satisfaction and Organizational Culture," Gallup, April 12, 2017, https://www.gallup.com/workplace/236366/right-culture-not -employee-satisfaction.aspx.

11. Fan Yang, Yao Jiang, and Xiaohong Pu, "Impact of Work Value Perception on Workers' Physical and Mental Health: Evidence from China," *Healthcare* 9, no. 8 (August 2021): 1059, https://doi.org/10.3390/healthcare9081059. PMID: 34442196; PMCID: PMC8393698.

12. Frank Martela, Marcos Gómez, Wenceslao Unanue, Sofia Araya, Diego Bravo, and Alvaro Espejo, "What Makes Work Meaningful? Longitudinal Evidence for the Importance of Autonomy and Beneficence for Meaningful Work," *Journal of Vocational Behavior* 131 (December 2021), https://doi.org/10.1016/j.jvb.2021.103631.

13. Martela et al., "What Makes Work Meaningful?"

14. Malcom Gladwell, *Outliers: The Story of Success* (New York: Little, Brown and Company, 2008).

15. Ferda Erdem and Janset Ozen, "Cognitive and Affective Dimensions of Trust in Developing Team Performance," *Team Performance Management* 9, no. 5/6 (2003): 131–135, https://doi .org/10.1108/13527590310493846.

16. Jason A. Colquitt, Brent A. Scott, and Jeffery A. LePine, "Trust, Trustworthiness, and Trust Propensity: A Meta-Analytic Test of Their Unique Relationships With Risk Taking and Job Performance," *Journal of Applied Psychology* 92, no. 4 (2007): 909–927, https://www.ocf .berkeley.edu/~reetaban/triple%20helix/trust%20and%20decision%20making.pdf.

17. Zeki Simsek, John F. Veiga, Michael H. Lubatkin, and Richard N. Dino, "Modeling the Multilevel Determinants of Top Management Team Behavioral Integration," *Academy of Management Journal* 48, no. 1 (2005): 69–84, https://doi.org/10.5465/AMJ.2005.15993139.

18. Simsek et al., "Modeling the Multilevel Determinants."

Chapter 2

1. Lizzie Duszynski-Goodman, "Mental Health Statistics and Facts," *Forbes*, February 21, 2024, https://www.forbes.com/health/mind/mental-health-statistics.

2. Jennifer Hemmerdinger, "New EY US Consulting Study: Employees Overwhelmingly Expect Empathy in the Workplace, But Many Say It Feels Disingenuous," EY, March 30, 2023, https://www.ey.com/en_us/newsroom/2023/03/new-ey-us-consulting-study#:~:text =About%20half%20(50%25%20and%2048,on%20how%20people%20show%20up.

3. Christine Porath, "The Hidden Toll of Workplace Incivility," *McKinsey Quarterly*, December 14, 2016, https://www.mckinsey.com/capabilities/people-and-organizational -performance/our-insights/the-hidden-toll-of-workplace-incivility?cid=soc-web.

4. Amy C. Edmondson, *The Fearless Organization: Creating Psychological Safety in the Workplace for Learning, Innovation, and Growth* (New York: John Wiley & Sons, 2018).

5. Korn Ferry, "The Korn Ferry Psychological Safety Index," 2024.

6. J. A. DiGirolamo and J. T. Tkach, "An Exploration of Managers and Leaders Using Coaching Skills," *Coaching Psychology Journal: Practice and Research* 71, no. 3 (2019): 195–218.

7. Hemmerdinger, "New EY US Consulting Study."

8. Naz Baheshti, "10 Timely Statistics About the Connection Between Employee Engagement and Wellness," *Forbes*, January 16, 2019, https://www.forbes.com/sites/nazbeheshti/2019/01 /16/10-timely-statistics-about-the-connection-between-employee-engagement-and-wellness /?sh=3e37288a22a0.

9. Jean Decety and Margarita Svetlova, "Putting Together Phylogenetic and Ontogenetic Perspectives on Empathy," *Developmental Cognitive Neuroscience* 2, no. 1 (January 2012): 1–24, https://doi.org/10.1016/j.dcn.2011.05.003.

10. Jane E. Dutton, Kristina M. Workman, and Ashley E. Hardin, "Compassion at Work," *The Annual Review of Organizational Behavior* (2014): 277–304, https://ideas.wharton.upenn.edu /wp-content/uploads/2018/07/Dutton-Workman-Hardman-2014.pdf.

11. Key details have been changed to preserve anonymity.

12. Kevin Cashman, *The Pause Principle: Step Back to Lead Forward* (Chicago: Berrett-Koehler, 2012).

13. B. K. Sahdra, K. A. MacLean, E. Ferrer, P. R. Shaver, E. L. Rosenberg, T. L. Jacobs, A. P. Zanesco, B. G. King, S. R. Aichele, D. A. Bridwell, G. R. Mangun, S. Lavy, B. A. Wallace, and C. D. Saron, "Enhanced Response Inhibition During Intensive Meditation Training Predicts Improvements in Self-Reported Adaptive Socioemotional Functioning," *Emotion* 11, no. 2 (2011): 299–312, https://doi.org/10.1037/a0022764.

14. Adam Lueke and Bryan Gibson, "Mindfulness Meditation Reduced Implicit Age and Race Bias," *Social Psychological and Personality Science* 6, no. 3 (November 2014), https://doi.org /10.1177/1948550614559651.

15. Joel A. DiGirolamo and Thomas J. Tkach, "An Exploration of Managers and Leaders Using Coaching Skills," *Consulting Psychology Journal: Practice and Research* 71, no. 3 (2019): 195–218, https://doi.org/10.1037/cpb0000138.

16. Tasha Eurich, "Working with People Who Aren't Self-Aware," *Harvard Business Review*, October 19, 2018, https://hbr.org/2018/10/working-with-people-who-arent-self-aware.

17. Eurich, "Working with People."

18. Tasha Eurich, *Insight: Why We're Not as Self-Aware as We Think, and How Seeing Ourselves Clearly Helps Us Succeed at Work and in Life* (New York: Crown Currency, 2018).

Chapter 3

1. Tom Langen, "Why Do Flocks of Birds Swoop and Swirl Together in the Sky? A Biologist Explains the Science of Murmurations," *Big Think* (blog), March 31, 2022, https://bigthink.com/life/murmurations.

2. Steven Sloman and Philip Fernbach, *The Knowledge Illusion: Why We Never Think Alone* (New York: Riverhead Books, 2017).

3. Nadia Drake, "First-ever Picture of a Black Hole Unveiled," *National Geographic*, April 10, 2019, https://www.nationalgeographic.com/science/article/first-picture-black-hole-revealed-m87-event-horizon-telescope-astrophysics.

4. "Black Holes: The Edge of All We Know," directed by Peter Galison (2020; Sandbox Films, Collapsar).

5. Hannah Critchlow, *Joined-Up Thinking: The Science of Collective Intelligence and Its Power to Change Our Lives* (London: Hodder & Stoughton, 2022).

6. For more on this, we recommend David Kantor's book *Reading the Room*, which offers valuable communication frameworks and tips for leaders and teams.

7. "The Science of Drumming and Synchronizing" excerpts from various studies:

Study 1: Tao Liu, Lian Duan, Ruina Dai, Matthew Pelowski, and Chaozhe Zhu, "Team-work, Team-brain: Exploring Synchrony and Team Interdependence in a Nine-Person Drumming Task via Multiparticipant Hyperscanning and Inter-Brain Network Topology with fNIRS," *Neuroimage* **237 (2021): 118–147, https://doi.org/10.1016/j.neuroimage.2021.118147.**

"The behavioral data revealed a higher level of drumming synchrony in the Team-focus condition where participants were asked to willfully try to synch their actions to the team, compared to the random condition, in which participants were asked to just drum as they wished, as well as the Shared-focus condition in which participants were asked to all pay attention to one external metronome to guide their drumming. This was concomitant with a higher level of perceived synchrony success and felt interdependence as recorded via self-reports from members of the teams. This finding alone is important that it reveals one more bit of support for the importance of interdependence on the success (in this case coherent drumming) of a team, suggesting that individuals work together better, and feel they have more cohesion, when they are actively attending to and modulating their actions based on those of the team, versus even an external cue, suggesting the importance of this factor in teamwork."

Study 2: Sebastian Kirschner and Michael Tomasello, "Joint Drumming: Social Context Facilitates Synchronization in Preschool Children," *Journal of Experimental Child Psychology* **102, no. 3 (2009): 299–314, https://doi.org/10.1016/j.jecp.2008.07.005.**

"Drumming together with a social partner creates a shared representation of the joint action task and/or elicits a specific human motivation to synchronize movements during joint rhythmic activity . . . The presence of a play partner should increase the motivation of the children to join in with the shared activity of drumming and/or facilitate the understanding of the joint action task by sharing its mental representation with the experimenter through joint attention."

Study 3: Idil Kokal, Annerose Engel, Sebastian Kirschner, and Christian Keysers, "Synchronized Drumming Enhances Activity in the Caudate and Facilitates Prosocial Commitment—If the Rhythm Comes Easily," *PLoS ONE* **6, no. 11 (2011), https://doi.org/10.1371/journal.pone.0027272.**

"We hypothesized that areas of the brain associated with the processing of reward would be active when individuals experience synchrony during drumming, and that these reward signals would increase prosocial behavior toward this synchronous drum partner . . . By showing an overlap in activated areas during synchronized drumming and monetary reward, our findings suggest that interpersonal synchrony is related to the brain's reward system."

Study 4: Ilanit Gordon, Avi Gilboa, Shai Cohen, Nir Milstein, Nir Haimovich, Shay Pinhasi, and Shahar Siegman, "Physiological and Behavioral Synchrony Predict Group Cohesion and Performance," *Scientific Reports* 10, no. 8484 (2020), https://doi.org/10.1038/s41598-020-65670-1.

"Our results highlight the importance of physiological and behavioral mechanisms of synchronization that support the development of group cohesion and performance. Using an ecologically valid real-life group setting via a novel synchronous vs. asynchronous musical paradigm, we showed that a manipulation in behavioral synchrony and emerging physiological coordination in IBI between group members predicted an enhanced sense of cohesion among group members.

"These findings have several important implications. First, they build on the large volume of previous work on interpersonal synchrony from the dyadic level and extend it to the group level. We gained an understanding of how synchrony, in different modalities, is associated with cohesion, resulting in coordinated performance in a complex group system. Second, noting that behavioral synchrony and physiological synchrony are both unique and independent predictors of group cohesion, we now have a more precise understanding of the distinct avenues by which group therapies or interventions can work.

"Since synchronous drumming is frequently used in group music therapy to enhance feelings of 'togetherness' and cohesion such clinical work can benefit from the physiological augmentation of the phenomenon investigated in this study."

Study 5: Michael Winkelman, "Complementary Therapy for Addiction: 'Drumming Out Drugs,'" *American Journal of Public Health* 93, no. 4 (2003): 647–651, https://doi.org/10.2105%2Fajph.93.4.647.

"Drumming produces physiological, psychological, and social stimulation that enhances recovery processes. Drumming induces relaxation and produces natural pleasurable experiences, enhanced awareness of preconscious dynamics, a release of emotional trauma, and reintegration of self. Drumming addresses self-centeredness, isolation, and alienation, creating a sense of connectedness with self and others. Drumming provides a secular approach to accessing a higher power and applying spiritual perspectives to the psychological and emotional dynamics of addiction. Drumming circles have important roles as complementary addiction therapy, particularly for repeated relapse and when other counseling modalities have failed. Drumming may reduce addiction by providing natural alterations of consciousness. Drumming groups may also aid recovery by enhancing health through their effects on social support and social networks."

8. Winkelman, "Complementary Therapy for Addiction."

9. Viola Spolin, *Theater Games for the Classroom: A Teacher's Handbook* (Evanston, IL: Northwestern University Press, 1986).

10. Bill Coffin, "The Science of Cartoon Thinking: Proving That Making People Laugh Can Transform the World," *Ethisphere Magazine*, August 14, 2023, https://magazine.ethisphere.com/the-science-of-cartoon-thinking-proving-that-making-people-laugh-can-transform-the-world.

11. "Are You One Of The World's Most Ethical Companies?" World's Most Ethical Companies, https://ethisphere.com/what-we-do/worlds-most-ethical-companies.

12. Michael Platt, *The Leader's Brain: Enhance Your Leadership, Build Stronger Teams, Make Better Decisions, and Inspire Greater Innovation with Neuroscience* (Philadelphia: Wharton School Press, 2020).

Chapter 4

1. We prefer the term cultural "dexterity" because "competence" leans more on awareness and knowledge, whereas dexterity leans more on the actions of situational adaptability premised on self- and other-awareness.

2. Marianna Pogosyan, "How Culture Shapes Emotions," *Psychology Today*, March 30, 2018, https://www.psychologytoday.com/us/blog/between-cultures/201803/how-culture-shapes -emotions; Marianna Pogosyan, "How Culture Wires Our Brains," *Psychology Today*, January 26, 2017, https://www.psychologytoday.com/us/blog/between-cultures/201701/how -culture-wires-our-brains; "Emotional Processing Influences by Culture and Language," *Neuroscience News*, February 15, 2024, https://neurosciencenews.com/emotional-processing -language-culture-25617; Ala Yankouskaya, Toby Denholm-Smith, Dewei Yi, Andrew James Greenshaw, Bo Cao, and Jie Sui, "Neural Connectivity Underlying Reward and Emotion-Related Processing: Evidence From a Large-Scale Network Analysis," *Frontiers in Systems Neuroscience* (April 2022), https://doi.org/10.3389/fnsys.2022.833625.

3. Fons Trompenaars and Charles Hampden-Turner, *Riding the Waves of Culture: Understanding Diversity in Global Business* (New York: McGraw Hill, 2012).

4. Duolingo Team, "This Is the Most Confusing Workplace Jargon around the World," *Duolingo* (blog), June 13, 2023, https://blog.duolingo.com/state-of-jargon-report.

5. Rupak Bhattacharya, "Last Call For Phone Calls?" *Korn Ferry Briefings Magazine*, https:// www.kornferry.com/insights/briefings-magazine/issue-61/last-call-for-phone-calls.

6. This scenario and dialogue was constructed by the authors in prompting dialogue with ChatGPT.

Chapter 5

1. Chef de cuisine (executive chef), sous chef, pâtissier (pastry chef), saucier (sauce chef), poissonnier (fish chef), rôtisseur (roast chef), grillardin (grill chef), friturier (fry chef), entremetier (vegetable chef), boucher (butcher chef), garde manger (pantry chef), boulanger (baker), commis chef (junior chef), chef de partie (a station chef).

2. F. R. C. Wit, L. L. Greer, and K. A. Jehn, "The Paradox of Intragroup Conflict: A Meta-Analysis," *Journal of Applied Psychology* 92, no. 2 (2012): 360–290, https://doi.org/10.1037 /a0024844.

3. Steve W. J. Kozlowski and Bradford S. Bell, "Work Groups and Teams in Organizations," *Industrial and Organizational Psychology* 12 (2003): 333–375.

4. Jim Harter, "Employee Engagement vs. Employee Satisfaction and Organizational Culture," Gallup, August 13, 2022, https://www.gallup.com/workplace/236366/right-culture-not -employee-satisfaction.aspx.

5. Sofie L. Valk, Boris C. Bernhardt, Fynn-Mathis Trautwein, Anne Böckler, Philipp Kanske, Nicolas Guizard, D. Louis Collins, and Tania Singer, "Structural Plasticity of the Social Brain: Differential Change After Socio-Affective and Cognitive Mental Training," *Science Advances* 3, no. 10 (2017), https://www.science.org/doi/10.1126/sciadv.1700489.

6. Shane Safir, "Listening Dyads Can Transform Your Team," Edutopia, December 10, 2014, https://www.edutopia.org/blog/listening-dyads-transform-team-shane-safir.

7. "#Listening Research and Its Power with Associate Professor Guy Itzchakov," *Listening Superpower Podcast*, https://listeningalchemy.com/listen-in/listening-research-and-its-power -with-associate-professor-guy-itzchakov.

8. Tony Hsieh, *Delivering Happiness: A Path to Profits, Passion, and Purpose* (New York: Grand Central Publishing, 2013).

9. Geert Hofstede, *Culture's Consequences: Comparing Values, Behaviors, Institutions, and Organizations Across Nations* (Thousand Oaks, CA: SAGE Publications, 2001).

Chapter 8

1. Daniel Kahneman, *Thinking, Fast and Slow* (New York: Farrar, Straus and Giroux, 2013).

2. For multiple stories of innovation at the employee level see Sophie Hamblett, "Innovation at Work: 4 Real-World Examples That Get It Right," *Interact* (blog), February 28, 2024, https://www.interactsoftware.com/blog/innovation-at-work-examples.

3. Peter M. Senge, *The Fifth Discipline: The Art & Practice of The Learning Organization* (New York: Doubleday, 2006).

4. Jeremy Utley and Perry Klebahn, *Ideaflow: The Only Business Metric That Matters* (New York: Portfolio, 2022).

5. Charles A. O'Reilly III and Michael L. Tushman, "The Ambidextrous Organization," *Harvard Business Review*, April 2004, https://hbr.org/2004/04/the-ambidextrous-organization.

6. Sandy Saputo, "How Rihanna's Fenty Beauty Delivered 'Beauty for All'—And a Wake-Up Call to the Industry." Think with Google, June 2019, https://www.thinkwithgoogle.com/future-of-marketing/management-and-culture/diversity-and-inclusion/-fenty-beauty-inclusive-advertising.

7. L. H. Nishii, "The Benefits of Climate for Inclusion for Gender-Diverse Groups," *Academy of Management Journal* 56, no. 6: 1754–1774.

8. Haley Bridger, "Skin Tone and Pulse Oximetry," *Brigham and Women's Communications, Harvard Medical School*, July 14, 2022, https://hms.harvard.edu/news/skin-tone-pulse-oximetry.

9. "The World's First Deodorant Designed for People with Disabilities," *Unilever*, April 27, 2021, https://www.unilever.com/news/news-search/2021/the-worlds-first-deodorant-designed-for-people-with-disabilities.

10. "Introducing LEGO Braille Bricks," LEGO Braille Bricks, accessed July 12, 2024, https://www.legobraillebricks.com.

11. For more on how to be an inclusive leader, see Korn Ferry's The 5 Disciplines of Inclusive Leaders white paper and book: https://www.kornferry.com/insights/featured-topics/diversity-equity-inclusion/5-disciplines-of-inclusive-leaders.

Chapter 9

1. These are just some of the current roles where AI is already replacing the need for humans to do many of the tasks: bank tellers, customer service representatives, manufacturing workers, retail workers, administrative roles, data entry clerks, paralegals and legal assistants, accountants and auditors, insurance underwriters, and financial analysts. In some cases, it will likely lead to full role elimination; in others, the automation will free up the humans in those roles to work more efficiently and put their time toward more advanced thinking and skills. Further, new roles that don't exist today will emerge as society and business realizes the implications of the changes AI is bringing everywhere. Sourced from the following: Michael Chui, Susan Lund and Peter Gumbel, "How Will Automation Affect Jobs, Skills, and Wages?" McKinsey Global Institute, March 23, 2018, https://www.mckinsey.com/featured-insights/future-of-work/how-will-automation-affect-jobs-skills-and-wages; Ian Shine and Kate Whiting, "These Are the Jobs Most Likely To Be Lost—and Created—Because of AI," *World Economic Forum*, May 4, 2023, https://www.weforum.org/agenda/2023/05/jobs-lost-created-ai-gpt/#:~:text=URL%3A%20https%3A%2F%2Fwww.weforum.org%2Fagenda%2F2023%2F05%2Fjobs.

2. Harry West, "A Chain of Innovation The Creation of the Swiffer," *Research Technology Management* 57, no. 3 (May 2014), https://www.researchgate.net/publication/262574898_A_Chain_of_Innovation_The_Creation_of_Swiffer.

3. Coauthor Andrés Tapia is a member of JFF's board.

4. Howard Schultz and Dori Jones Yang, *Pour Your Heart Into It: How Starbucks Built a Company One Cup at a Time* (California: Hyperion, 1997).

5. Ray Oldenburg, *The Great Good Place: Cafes, Coffee Shops, Bookstores, Bars, Hair Salons, and Other Hangouts at the Heart of a Community* (Massachusetts: Da Capo Press, 1999).

Chapter 10

1. Curtis Bunn, "Diversity Officers Hired in 2020 Are Losing Their Jobs, and the Ones Who Remain Are Mostly White," *NBC News*, February 27, 2023, https://www.yahoo.com/news/hamstrung-golden-handcuffs-diversity-roles-194601215.html?guce_referrer=aHR0cHM6Ly93d3cuYmluZy5jb20v&guce_referrer_sig=AQAAAGMa-1EJ0BLx0uTYROH1zNHz7La-rdhH83pkFtG_j2MjjAOROZyJViVBfP4YCQDiTP0HACa3A8Jr5I-xZh42Gr6jZ8m_nXshetUdWvEwyCnqQOaIxzk1dZuQuQPTMY9rGc0dVgm6agoA_j42FqnGqLsP0zhx3fcEm3fpuxqbwmI2&guccounter=2.

2. "Diversity, Equity & Inclusion: Real Progress or Just for Show?" Korn Ferry Insights, https://www.kornferry.com/insights/featured-topics/diversity-equity-inclusion/global-dei -pulse-survey.

3. Aneesh Raman and Cat Ward, "The Next Era of Work Will Be About Skills—Not Pedigree. Here's How Employers Are Changing the Way They Judge Potential, According to LinkedIn and Jobs for the Future," *Forbes*, January 5, 2023, https://fortune.com/2023/01/05/next-era-of -work-skills-degree-jobs-raman-ward.

4. David Kenny, "The Future of Work Hinges on Skills, Not College Degrees," LinkedIn, May 17, 2022, https://www.linkedin.com/pulse/future-work-hinges-skills-college-degrees-david -kenny.

Appendix C

1. Steven Sloman and Philip Fernbach, *The Knowledge Illusion* (New York: Riverhead Books, 2018).

BIBLIOGRAPHY

Movies

2001: A Space Odyssey (1968)
Apollo 13 (1995)
Amélie (2001)
Captains of the World (re: Qatar World Cup) (2023)
Cool Runnings (1993)
Crouching Tiger, Hidden Dragon (2000)
Hidden Figures (2016)
Ocean's Eleven (2001)
Papillon (1973)
Remember the Titans (2000)
School of Rock (2003)
The Avengers (2012)
The Italian Job (2003)
The Last Dance (re: the six-time champion Chicago Bulls) (2020)

Books

An Everyone Culture: Becoming a Deliberately Developmental Organization by Robert Kegan and
 Lisa Laskow Lahey
Being More Creative: No Matter Where You Work by Kathryn Haydon
Brain-centric Design: The Surprising Neuroscience Behind Learning with a Deep Understanding by
 Rich Carr and Dr. Kieran O'Mahony
Dare to Lead: Brave Work. Tough Conversations. Whole Hearts by Brené Brown
*Daring Greatly: How the Courage to Be Vulnerable Transforms the Way We Live, Love, Parent, and
 Lead* by Brené Brown
Good to Great: Why Some Companies Make the Leap . . . and Others Don't by Jim Collins
Joined-Up Thinking: The Science of Collective Intelligence by Hannah Critchlow
Power and Prediction: The Disruptive Economics of Artificial Intelligence by Ajay Agrawal, Joshua
 Gans, and Avi Goldfarb
*The Fearless Organization: Creating Psychological Safety in the Workplace for Learning, Innovation,
 and Growth* by Amy Edmondson
The Fifth Discipline: The Art & Practice of The Learning Organization by Peter Senge
The Five Dysfunctions of a Team by Patrick Lencioni
The Ideal Team Player by Patrick Lencioni
The Wisdom of Teams by Jon R. Katzenbach and Douglas K. Smith

ACKNOWLEDGMENTS

A T KORN FERRY WE ARE A COLLECTION of Caring, Connecting, Synchronizing, Culturally Dexterous, and Powersharing inclusive teams as we every day, every hour, every minute go in and out of multiple teams of different sizes, with different purposes, spread out across multiple geographies.

It took various inclusive teams to pull this book together.

And within them, here are the team members we want to call out, because without you we don't get this done!

SUPER CONTRIBUTORS

THE KORN FERRY EDITORIAL TEAM

Research, Production, and Project Management

Stephanie Collins, Korn Ferry Consultant—You did it again! You have been part of the editorial team through the entirety of the Five Inclusive Disciplines trilogy. Each time, including in this latest book, you have contributed savvy research, strong writing, eagle-eyed in attention to detail. And you are simply a delight to work with every moment.

Samantha Agostino, Korn Ferry Consultant—Your first book project! You stepped in, and up, like a pro. Always on top of everything, making sure nothing fell through the cracks. And always unfazed no matter what was going on.

Trisha Messina, Executive Assistant—Without you, things would fall apart. With you, we soar. You are an elite EA. And the epitome of an inclusive team member.

Peer Reviewers

The intellectual gurus, the challengers—always on the quest for excellence:
Full Book:

- Barry Callender, MBA, Associate Client Partner
- Sarah Hezlett, PhD, VP Assessment Science, Korn Ferry Institute
- Karen Huang, PhD, Senior Director of Search Assessment

Selections:

- Amelia Haynes, Manager of Research and Partnership Development and cognitive science practitioner, Korn Ferry Institute
- Fayruz Kirtzman, Senior Client Partner, Global DE&I Diagnostic Solution Leader

CONTRIBUTORS

Thought Partners

The Inclusive Teams Solution Team: Anne Weinstein, David Williams, Jay Sukumaran, Jonida Xhaferraj, Laura Mancini, Laura Weiss, Mike Solomons, Ömer Ongun, and Steven D'Souza. We fully leveraged the diversity of the team in an inclusive way to generate the innovative thinking found here.

Thought leadership peer reviewer and collaborator: Alina Polonskaia, for her erudite scouring of the latest research and her differentiated way of thinking that was the stress test our emerging inclusive teams model required.

Pilot team: Michelle Stuntz, and her Korn Ferry team at the time, were our alpha pilots for testing out various of our hypotheses and interventions. That was a very generous gift of time you gave us.

The Korn Ferry Institute: Your massive body of research, your support in helping us track down findings, and your making Sarah Hezlett, Amelia Haynes, and Chloe Carr available to bring their neurological diversity to this project elevated the work. Thank you, Jean-Marc Laouchez, Tessa Misiaszek, and Annamarya Scaccia.

Additional Sidebar Authors: The Neuroscience Corner sequence (seven sidebars) by Amelia Haynes, "Caring for a Team Member with a Hidden Disability: When My Epilepsy Throws Me on the Floor" by Matt Norquist, Senior Partner, Korn Ferry; "How Cartoon Thinking Switched the Punch Line on Business Ethics Training" by Pat Byrnes, New Yorker cartoonist; "Narrowing the Cultural Communication Gap between Generations" by Chloe Carr [Researcher], Korn Ferry Institute; "Fenty Beauty: A Tapestry of Shades and Teamwork" by Stephanie Collins, Consultant, Korn Ferry.

It also takes partners inside and outside of Korn Ferry to get things done.

Editing

- Danielle Goodman, Developmental Editor
- Neal Maillet, Commissioning Editor, Berrett-Koehler Publishers

Production

- Stephanie Collins, MS and Samantha Agostino, Editorial and Project Management
- Lizzie Cave, photos and images
- Dan Tesser, Cover Designer
- Westchester Publishing Services, UK: Book Production
- Grace Weir: Production Editor
- Ashley Ingram, Art Director

Marketing

- Christy Kirk, Berrett-Koehler Publishers
- Lizzie Cave, Korn Ferry

To Our Families

Researching and, especially, writing can—for all our talk of teams—be quite the solitary task for long stretches of this collective endeavor. It's the one process that our families feel the effect of the most, as the writing takes us away from them. We both are grateful that our families understand what drives us—and that we need to get our ideas out. Throughout this long project, they continually provided us the space to imagine and create. ¡Gracias! Merci! Thank you!—*Andrés*

■   ■   ■

INDEX

Note: Information in figures and tables is indicated by f and t.

ABOUT THE AUTHORS

Andrés Tapia

is a Senior Client Partner and is Korn Ferry's Global Diversity
and Inclusion Strategist.

Andrés has been one of the leading voices in
shaping a contemporary, next-generation
approach to diversity and inclusion. The approach is global, deeply integrated into talent
systems, and focused on enabling marketplace
success. He has over twenty-five years of experience as a C-suite management consultant,
diversity executive, organizational development
and training professional, and journalist.

Throughout Europe, Asia, North America, and his native Latin America, Andrés has served clients in shaping their enterprise-wide diversity
and inclusion business cases and strategies across industries—including
financial, technology, health care, retail, manufacturing, government,
not-for-profits, and education—with dozens of Global 500 organizations as
well as non-US multinationals in Brazil, South Korea, and India.

Andrés is the author of the groundbreaking book *The Inclusion
Paradox: The Obama Era and the Transformation of Global Diversity*, as
well as the coauthor of *Auténtico: The Definitive Guide to Latino Career
Success*, *The 5 Disciplines of Inclusive Leadership: Unleashing the Power of
All of Us*, and *The 5 Disciplines of Inclusive Organizations: How Diverse
and Equitable Enterprises Will Transform the World*. He's a frequently
sought-after speaker globally on the topic of diversity and inclusion. He
has been published in major dailies throughout the United States and
Latin America, mainly through his writing for the New America Media
wire service and on the Huffington Post.

He is the recipient of numerous leadership and diversity awards and is currently serving on the boards of Jobs for the Future, Leadership Greater Chicago, Ravinia Festival, The Gaylord and Dorothy Donnelley Foundation, and Working Together. He previously served as a Commissioner on the Highland Park (IL) Housing Commission overseeing that city's Inclusionary Housing code. He now serves in an elected position as Highland Park city council member. He began his four-year term on May 10, 2021.

Andrés received a bachelor's degree in modern history from Northwestern University with an emphasis in journalism and political science. He grew up in a bilingual/bicultural home in Lima, Perú. He is married to Lori, a musician, and their grown daughter, Marisela, is a professional flamenco performer and choreographer.

https://www.linkedin.com/in/andrestapia1/

Michel Buffet, PhD

is a Senior Client Partner and is Korn Ferry's Top Team Solutions Leader.

Michel partners with C-suite leaders and human resources practitioners on organizational and talent development solutions designed to unlock the performance potential of individual executives, leadership teams, and organizations.

He has over twenty-five years of consulting experience in C-suite succession, leadership assessment, executive development and coaching, high-performance team development, and organizational transformation.

Michel is Korn Ferry's Top Team Performance Solution Leader and is a member of the CEO & Board Services practice. He is also the advisory lead on several of the firm's key accounts across industries, including Consumer Products, Life Science, and Professional Services.

Prior to joining Korn Ferry, Michel was managing consultant and head of leadership resilience at YSC. Prior to this, he was an owner and managing partner at Fisher Rock Consulting and a partner at Oliver Wyman Delta. He started his career as an Officer Psychologist in the French Navy.

He is a board member at French American Chamber of Commerce in New York (FACC-NY) where he chairs the HR & Mobility Committee.

He is the former president and board member of the Metropolitan New York Association of Applied Psychology and an active member of the Society of Industrial and Organizational Psychology. He is also a board member of NextGen Leaders, assisting in developing high potential leaders in the LGBTQ+ community. He has authored several articles on executive onboarding and organizational applications of Social Network Analysis (SNA).

He holds a PhD in organizational psychology from Columbia University and a doctorate in clinical psychology from the University of Paris. He is a French and American citizen and is bilingual in French and English and fluent in Spanish. He lives in Princeton, New Jersey.

https://www.linkedin.com/in/michelbuffet/

ABOUT KORN FERRY

Korn Ferry is a global organizational consulting firm. We work with our clients to design optimal organization structures, roles, and responsibilities.

We help them hire the right people and advise them on how to reward and motivate their workforce while developing professionals as they navigate and advance their careers.

Related to the content in this book, Korn Ferry has one of the most transformational top team, team optimization, and DE&I practices and solutions globally.

To learn how we can help you on your perform and transform journey:

Contact us at:
https://www.kornferry.com/contact

KORN FERRY
Business advisors.
Career makers.

Kornferry.com

Berrett–Koehler
Publishers

Berrett-Koehler is an independent publisher dedicated to an ambitious mission: *Connecting people and ideas to create a world that works for all.*

Our publications span many formats, including print, digital, audio, and video. We also offer online resources, training, and gatherings. And we will continue expanding our products and services to advance our mission.

We believe that the solutions to the world's problems will come from all of us, working at all levels: in our society, in our organizations, and in our own lives. Our publications and resources offer pathways to creating a more just, equitable, and sustainable society. They help people make their organizations more humane, democratic, diverse, and effective (and we don't think there's any contradiction there). And they guide people in creating positive change in their own lives and aligning their personal practices with their aspirations for a better world.

And we strive to practice what we preach through what we call "The BK Way." At the core of this approach is *stewardship*, a deep sense of responsibility to administer the company for the benefit of all of our stakeholder groups, including authors, customers, employees, investors, service providers, sales partners, and the communities and environment around us. Everything we do is built around stewardship and our other core values of *quality*, *partnership*, *inclusion*, and *sustainability.*

This is why Berrett-Koehler is the first book publishing company to be both a B Corporation (a rigorous certification) and a benefit corporation (a for-profit legal status), which together require us to adhere to the highest standards for corporate, social, and environmental performance. And it is why we have instituted many pioneering practices (which you can learn about at www.bkconnection.com), including the Berrett-Koehler Constitution, the Bill of Rights and Responsibilities for BK Authors, and our unique Author Days.

We are grateful to our readers, authors, and other friends who are supporting our mission. We ask you to share with us examples of how BK publications and resources are making a difference in your lives, organizations, and communities at www.bkconnection.com/impact.

Dear reader,

Thank you for picking up this book and welcome to the worldwide BK community! You're joining a special group of people who have come together to create positive change in their lives, organizations, and communities.

What's BK all about?

Our mission is to connect people and ideas to create a world that works for all.

Why? Our communities, organizations, and lives get bogged down by old paradigms of self-interest, exclusion, hierarchy, and privilege. But we believe that can change. That's why we seek the leading experts on these challenges—and share their actionable ideas with you.

A welcome gift

To help you get started, we'd like to offer you a **free copy** of one of our bestselling ebooks:

www.bkconnection.com/welcome

When you claim your **free ebook**, you'll also be subscribed to our blog.

Our freshest insights

Access the best new tools and ideas for leaders at all levels on our blog at ideas.bkconnection.com.

Sincerely,

Your friends at Berrett-Koehler

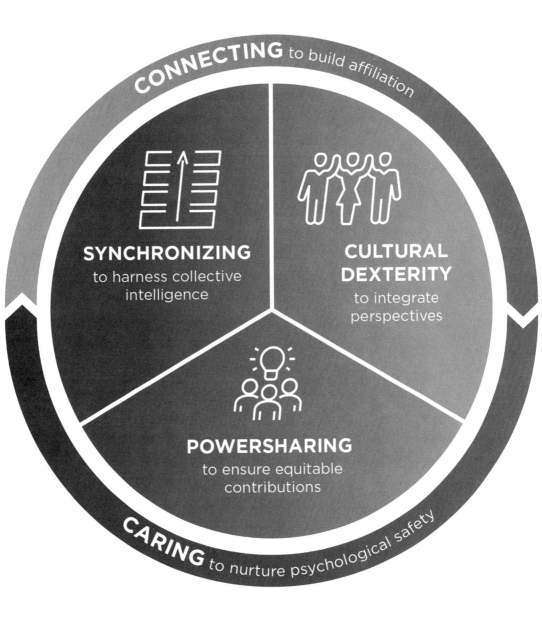

The Inclusive™ Teams model.

Source: Korn Ferry, 2025.